Orature in
African Literature Today
18

African Literature Today

Editor: Eldred Durosimi Jones
* 1, 2, 3 and 4 Omnibus Edition
  5 The Novel in Africa
  6 Poetry in Africa
  7 Focus on Criticism
  8 Drama in Africa
* 9 Africa, America
  & the Caribbean
*10 Retrospect & Prospect
 11 Myth & History

Editor: Eldred Durosimi Jones
Associate Editor: Eustace Palmer
Assistant Editor: Marjorie Jones
 12 New Writing, New Approaches
*13 Recent Trends in the Novel
*14 Insiders and Outsiders
1–14 were published from London by
Heinemann Educational Books and from
New York by Africana Publishing
Company

*Copies of back issues marked with an asterisk may be purchased from your book-
seller or direct from James Currey Ltd

The new series is published by
James Currey Publishers and Africa World Press
*ALT 15 Women in African Literature Today
*ALT 16 Oral & Written Poetry in African Literature Today
*ALT 17 The Question of Language in African Literature Today
ALT 18 Orature in African Literature Today
ALT 19 Critical Theories & African Literature Today
The deadline for articles has passed
ALT 20 New Writers in African Literature Today
The deadline for articles is 30 June 1993

*Published   Place a standing order with your supplier for future issues

Future Issues

ALT 19 *Critical Theories & African Literature Today* will be on the theme of critical
theories and their application to African literature. Articles can examine the
relevance of structuralism, deconstruction, marxism, feminism, post-modernism,
black aesthetics and traditional criticism to African literature in general,
individual authors or particular works.

ALT 20 *New Writers in African Literature Today* will examine the works of writers
who have appeared (or have developed significantly) in the last two decades in any
of the genres.

Before embarking on articles contributors are advised to submit proposals to the
Editor, Professor Eldred Durosimi Jones; Fourah Bay College, University of Sierra
Leone, PO Box 87, Freetown, Sierra Leone. Unsolicited articles are welcome, but
will not be returned unless adequate postage arrangements are made by the
contributors.

All articles should be well typed, double spaced on A4 paper with a wide margin.
References to books should include the author or editor, place, publisher, date and
the relevant pages.
Contributors must keep a spare copy in case of loss in transit.

Orature in
African Literature Today

A review
Editor: ELDRED DUROSIMI JONES
Associate Editor: EUSTACE PALMER
Assistant Editor: MARJORIE JONES

Africa World Press, Inc.
P.O. Box 1892
Trenton, New Jersey 08607

Africa World Press, Inc.
P.O. Box 1892
Trenton, NJ 08607

First Africa World Press Edition 1992

Library of Congress Catalog Card Number: 70-2505

ISBN:

        0-86543-350-X   CLOTH
        0-86543-351-8   PAPER

ISSN Number: 0065-4000

Published in England by:

JAMES CURREY LTD.
54b Thornhill Square
Islington, London N1 1BE

Contents

v

vi   Contents

Editorial Article
Myth & Modernity:
African Writers & their Roots

Eldred D. Jones

Life on the African continent is greatly influenced by the multiplicity of ethnic groups each defined principally by its distinctive language. Roughly seven hundred and fifty languages have been identified in the continent. One of the most populous states, Nigeria, has about four hundred languages and one of the smallest, Sierra Leone has seventeen.[1]

Perhaps the most serious obstacle to national development within states is the effect of conflicts and rivalries between ethnic groups, and the failure of national governments to harness the diverse groups and direct them towards common ideals. The ethnic groups are rich with cultural energy and strong in corporate will which if properly channelled would work to the good of the nations. In most African nations, however, the ideal of national unity out of cultural diversity is still a distant one.

Before the advent of European colonialism in the nineteenth century, through trade, war and politics, some ethnic groups had become associated in imperial and other coalitions and some languages had evolved as dominant giving access to centres of power. The great Zulu coalition under Shaka, the empires of Mali, Songhai and Ghana, exemplify such groupings. At the coming of European colonialism, strong central governments imposed an imperial European language over large areas inhabited by distinctive tribal language groups. These new arbitrary borders have divided families, as rival colonial powers drew lines through their ancestral affiliations. Thus Camara Laye in Guinea wrote in French while Sarif Easmon in neighbouring Sierra Leone writes in English though they share very similar ethnic roots. The arbitrary boundaries of the colonial era have been inherited by the new African states along with one or other of the colonial languages, now mainly English, French and Portuguese, spread thinly over a multiplicity of ethnic languages and cultures. It is in these African cultures – the tribal cultures – that all African writers have their base. (I have used all, but it might be argued that there are at least the beginnings of urban based cultures with only loose tribal associations but these are, if they can be identified, still very much in their infancy).

African literature is still tribally based, and derives its strength from

1

tribal sources. Yet most serious African writing today is in one or other of the learnt colonial languages. Some African writers, notably Ngũgĩ wa Thiong'o, have now taken a conscious decision to write in their ethnic language – Ngũgĩ in Kikuyu – but this is still very much a minority movement among major African writers even though the theoretical case for writing African literature in African languages has been argued loud and long. The writers have voted eloquently with their pens.

If African writers write from their ethnic base, it is fortunate that this is usually very rich and the best writers exploit the resources of their base for ideas, themes and other linguistic influences. It needs to be said that although most indigenous African languages are still used mainly for oral communication, many of them have, for centuries, been vehicles for oral artistic verbal composition and transmission now formalised by the term 'orature'. Over the last three decades there have been serious attempts at collecting, translating and publishing orally transmitted narratives, poems and songs. Examples of these appeared in *The Oxford Library of African Literature*, edited by E.E. Evans-Pritchard, W.H. Whiteley and Godfrey Leinhardt.[2]

More recently, J.P. Clark produced his translation and reconstruction of the Ozidi play.[3] The Ewe dirges have been similarly studied and, a further advance used as inspiration for his modern poetry by Kofi Awoonor whose poetry is examined in the article by Isaac Elimimian. This use of the African ethnic tradition by modern African writers is explored in various articles in this issue. Poetic recitation is the most continuous of the genres and traditional poetic forms have therefore, not surprisingly, quite significantly influenced the work of modern African poets, some of whom made a study of their particular traditions and then quite deliberately imitated their form and style in their own compositions. Kofi Awoonor published the result of his study of the poetic forms of the Ewe in *Guardians of the Sacred Word: Ewe Poetry* – a collection containing his English translations of these oral recitations.[4] His own poetry in which he quite often laments the loss of African values is written in the style of these dirges even though they carry contemporary themes.[5] J.P. Clark transmits through his poetry the values of Ijaw traditional life and some of his best lyric poetry – 'Night Rain', 'For Granny (From Hospital)' for example – are poignant evocations of Ijaw traditional life. His most substantial volume however is the result of fifteen years study of *The Ozidi Saga*, an Ijaw traditional drama cycle. It is easy to see why Clark's own poetry so eloquently evokes Ijaw traditional life. Yet this poetry ranges far and wide taking in modern political themes drawn from the Nigerian Federation and the Civil War.[6]

A similar thread which links the traditional and the modern is seen in the poetry of Okot p'Bitek; he completed his thesis *Oral Literature and its Background among the Acoli and Lang'o* at the Institute of Social Anthropology in Oxford in 1964. He then took the whole African continent by storm when he published in direct imitation of these traditional 'songs' his *Song of Lawino*[7] which he had in fact first written and published in the Acoli language. Thus perhaps the most popular volume of poetry ever published in Africa – it remains a best-seller – is directly imitative of the poetic form of an African tribe. p'Bitek followed *Song of Lawino* with *Song of Ocol*,[8] 'Song of Malaya'[9] and 'Song of Prisoner'[10] all in the same style but all concerned with contemporary modern themes.

Such stylistic influences can be seen even in the work of prose writers. The use of such devices in poetry is not perhaps unexpected, the poetic tradition being the most continuous of the genres. These influences are also to be seen in the work of playwrights whose incorporation of folk material – songs, dances and rituals – is commonplace. Even the novelists however look for stylistic influences from their tribal roots. Chinua Achebe is the acknowledged 'old master' in this tradition.[11] *Things Fall Apart*[12] led a whole movement involving Flora Nwapa (examined in this issue), Elechi Amadi, Onuora Nzekwu and others, and Achebe himself has deftly deployed these sources in every novel right up to *Anthills of the Savannah*.[13] Ayi Kwei Armah in *The Healers*,[14] has used the technique of the traditional story-teller as his overall structural device and the flow of the narrative is punctuated at significant points with invocations. As the narrator proceeds to itemize the sadistic details of the murder and disfigurement of Prince Appia, he exclaims:

Ah, Fasseke, words fail the story-teller.
Fasseke Belen Tigui, master of masters
in the art of eloquence, lend me strength.
Send me eloquence to finish what I have begun. (p. 63)

The effect is to emphasise the extreme brutality and savagery of the murder, but also to excuse the recital of other such disgusting details, a mitigating device not employed by Armah in other novels where equally gory details are recounted using more conventional novelistic structures. His use of oral traditional material in his short stories is examined by Ode Ogede later in this issue.

Both in form and substance, the folktale has influenced the work of contemporary writers. Niyi Osundare, one of the foremost of the new generation of Nigerian poets, uses the folktale form (along with more poetic forms like the *oriki*) as a vehicle for poetic satire in, for example, *Village Voices*.[15] (For an examination of his use of folk material, see Aderemi Bamikunle pp. 49–61). The folk motif of the girl who refuses all eligible suitors to marry a complete stranger who later turns into a devil is found in treatments as varied as Amos Tutuola's 'curious creature who turned into a skull'[16] and Ama Ata Aidoo's *Anowa*[17] to Syl Cheney-Coker's *The Last Harmattan of Alusine Dunbar*.[18]

It has been pointed out how Soyinka in his plays often uses the town festival, a feature of Yoruba life, as an overall structural device: *A Dance of the Forests, The Swamp Dwellers, The Strong Breed,*[19] *Kongi's Harvest,*[20] *Death and the King's Horseman,*[21] all show this feature of a festival providing Soyinka with the framework for his plays.[22]

A different attempt to use the oral heritage in a contemporary work is Gabriel Okara's reconstruction of English syntax to give the language of his novel *The Voice,*[23] an African ring. This is a more thorough-going effort to achieve an effect for which many African authors strive, namely to incorporate expressions, proverbs etc., from their own languages to flavour their borrowed languages.

Yet most African writers, even though they use ethnic material for both linguistic and thematic inspiration, are often concerned with much wider applications. Apart from providing an illustration of the stylistic influence of traditional forms on a contemporary writer using English, *The Healers* also shows Armah using the ethnic setting as a base from which to treat continental and even global concerns.

The Healers is set in Esuano, a part of the now fragmented Asante kingdom, its fragmentation from selfishness being used as an image of the disunity and consequent weakness of the black race, 'Ebibirman'. The novel depicts the life of one small fragment of the once great whole, and painstakingly pictures life in the village – its sports, feasts, crimes, its calculating manipulators through whose machinations people are divided, as well as its 'healers' whose influences would piece together the scattered elements and restore unity and wholeness, not just to the fragmented Asante, but – and this is the point – to the entire black race:

> There will always be work for healers, even when the highest work is done. That highest work, the bringing together again of the black people, will take centuries. You, Densu growing up, have been told you belong to the Fantse people, like everyone else at Esuano. No one told you the Fantse people are no people at all but a single small fragment of one community that misfortune blew apart. Of that exploded community the Asante are also a part. The Denchira, the Akim, the Wassa, the Sewhi, the Aowin, the Nzema, the Ekuapem – all these are merely scattered pieces of what once came together.
>
> Not only that. The Akan community itself was just a little piece of something whole – a people that knew only this one name we so seldom hear these days: Ebibirman. That was the community of all black people. (pp. 101–2)

From the micro-scene of a conversation in Esuano between the healer, Damfo, and Densu in the presence of Araba Jesiwa, the horizon of the novel spreads not only to the whole Asante people but to the whole black race which once, according to Damfo, was also united. A similar, but not so explicitly depicted radiation outwards from the micro-centre, can be seen in Armah's other novels to varying degrees.[24] Derek Wright in this issue examines Armah's manipulation, even fictionalisation, of history in *Two Thousand Seasons.*

In Soyinka's *The Swamp Dwellers,* the blind beggar from the drought-stricken north travels south to the flooded riverine areas where he encounters the whole ethnic paraphernalia – fat priest, the snake-god, carefully fostered superstitions – all combining to keep the people starving and backward in the midst of potential plenty. It is the man from the barren north, blind to boot, who seems destined to rescue the doomed south. Through this startlingly ironical portrayal, Soyinka in this early play is, like Armah in his novel, concerned with the clash and possible reconcilement of ethnic groups whose unity in common purpose is the path to nationhood.

Mazisi Kunene in his modern epic realization of the Shaka legend, examined later by Wole Ogundele, deliberately sets out to 'correct' the usual European picture of the Zulu hero. Femi Osofisan actually subverts the traditional myths to make them serve his own egalitarian purposes (see Muyiwa Awodiya's article, 'Oral Literature and Modern Nigerian Drama'), while other authors, Flora Nwapa for example, are more conservative in their treatment of the traditional oral lore (see John Conteh-Morgan and Chidi Ikonné).

The city is the melting pot of ethnicity, and African writers have in their urban novels treated this theme in various ways since Ekwensi's pioneering *People of the City*.[25] Soyinka's five interpreters flitting between Lagos and Ibadan, and occasionally returning to their ethnic bases, are united by a common educational background; their common interest in art, literature and life, and in their conflicts and compromises with themselves and with the still unformed whirlpool of Nigerian political and social life, point the way towards the uncertain future of the new Nigeria. Soyinka's base is the Yoruba civilisation. The landscapes, the cosmology, religion and social patterns and the language are basic sources of his imagery and the metaphor for his themes, but these then far exceed in their treatment and application their immediate provenance. The central event in *Kongi's Harvest* is the New Yam Festival. It symbolises the humane system of political organisation which has its roots in the corporate will of the people, a system which has been almost displaced by the ruthless tyrannical rule of Kongi, the new-style African dictator. In spite of its vulnerability to the weapons of Kongi – guns and propaganda – the old regime is ethically superior. Kongi realises this and wishes to annex the spiritual authority of the old regime. But as the play suggests, there are no short cuts to spiritual authority; it has to be earned. Kongi has to face the grim fact that he can only retain power by the means which first gave it to him – blood. Thus through the local metaphor of the New Yam, Soyinka presents a theme of universal significance.

African writers derive their original inspiration from their culture bases but they have also at their disposal the whole Western literary tradition. I have referred earlier to the rich oral tradition which is a part of the ethnic cultures of Africa, and which has provided both thematic and stylistic inspiration for writers. The actual forms – fiction, poetry and drama – show the double heritage. Narrative is, for example, an art long practised in Africa, but the prose novel is a modern form borrowed and adapted by African writers. Drama similarly has its African roots but the stage play, while being very African in material shows heavy influence from the Western theatre tradition. Ola Rotimi and Wole Soyinka have worked from the opposite starting point in two of their plays. In *The Gods are Not to Blame*,[26] Rotimi uses what is after all Greek folk material, universalised by Sophocles in *Oedipus Tyrannus*, and, giving it an African setting brings it alive for African theatregoers. Oedipus' fatal assurance is deftly translated in King Odewale's imperious pride in his tribe which precipitates his crime, and the irony is fully realized when it is revealed to him that he was mistaken even in his tribal identity. Wole Soyinka similarly turns Euripides' *The Bacchae* inside out to bring its message home. He saw the similarity between the Greek god Dionysos who had in his nature more than a touch of waywardness and the Yoruba god Ogun who blindly slaughtered his own subjects – the men of Ire. He sees the opportunity to look at the theme of internecine strife which was so topical in Nigeria through this seemingly remote tradition of Greek mythology.

Although African writers draw inspiration from their particular ethnic bases, their ultimate vision is national, even global.

The ethnic background offers them the metaphor for their vision. What the writers see around them as they survey their political and social environment since independence is a recurring cycle of misrule, mismanagement, corruption, violent upheaval and general misery. It is interesting that in looking to the future, some of the most hard-headed novelists take a backward glance at the cohesion which characterised the small ethnic societies. This is not in the best of them mere stagnant nostalgia but a search for an ethic nurtured within a small idealistic community and spread by means of a moral revolution throughout the nation and even more widely. Ngũgĩ, Soyinka and Armah in their recent work offer different examples of dynamic new groups, the new tribes – but not ethnically exclusive – which are the sources of this revolution. In Ngũgĩ's *Petals of Blood*[27] the citizens of Il Morog, an instant township on the fringes of the great city, are moulded together by their misery, the combined result of economic exploitation and drought, and they become a new force out of which a terrible beauty might emerge. The citizens of Il Morog were not a tribe in the strict ethnic sense. They were a peri-urban conglomerate – an environmental blot, out of which the new revolutionary spirit will come. Wole Soyinka in his *Season of Anomy*[28] presents a group, the community of Aiyero, which seeks its motivation from the coherence and the wholeness of the tribal vision. The peace and tranquillity of the Aiyero setting, its suggestion of genuine African authenticity is contrasted with the obscene ostentation of the governing Cartel, the embodiment of political and economic corruption.

This same type of movement has been already illustrated in Armah's

The Healers, but it is also the informing idea in *Two Thousand Seasons*. These writers do not present an easy ride out of all Africa's troubles. These movements of the future are portrayed as frail, tender growths striving to spread in the face of the most formidable of obstacles. In Soyinka's final glance at his group in *Season of Anomy*, they are a battered, defeated band hobbling back to their base, in the hope of recovering their strength for perhaps another attempt against the tremendous odds of national corruption. Is Africa's hope to be the ethic of the new tribes?

NOTES

1. Hansford et al., *An Index of Nigerian Languages* (Accra: Summer Institute of Linguistics, 1976); G. Ansre, *Language Policy for the Promotion of National Unity and Understanding in West Africa* (Legon: Institute of African Studies, 1970).
2. H.F. Morris, *The Heroic Recitations of the Bahima of Ankole* (1964); I. Schapera, *Praise Poems of Tswana Chiefs* (1965); G.W.B. Huntingford, *The Glorious Victories of Amda Seyon* (1965); H.A.S. Johnston, *A Selection of Hausa Stories* (1966); John Mbiti, *Akamba Stories* (1966); S.A. Babalola, *The Content and Form of Ijala* (1966); all published by Oxford Clarendon Press.
3. J.P. Clark, *The Ozidi Saga* (Ibadan: Ibadan University Press in association with OUP, 1977).
4. Kofi Awoonor, *Guardians of the Sacred Word: Ewe Poetry* (New York: Nok Publishers, 1974).
5. Kofi Awoonor, *Rediscovery and Other Poems* (Ibadan: Mbari, 1964).
6. J.P. Clark, *Casualties: Poems 1966/68* (London: Longman, 1970, 2nd edition, 1979; New York: Africana Publishing Corporation, 1970).
7. Okot p'Bitek, *Song of Lawino* (Nairobi: EAPH, 1966).
8. Okot p'Bitek, *Song of Ocol* (Nairobi: EAPH, 1970).
9. Okot p'Bitek, 'Song of Malaya', *Two Songs* (Nairobi: EAPH, 1971).
10. Okot p'Bitek, 'Song of Prisoner', *Two Songs* (Nairobi: EAPH, 1971).
11. See for example Bernth Lindfors, 'The Palm Oil with which Achebe's Words are Eaten', *African Literature Today*, 1 (1968).
12. Chinua Achebe, *Things Fall Apart* (London: Heinemann, 1958).
13. Chinua Achebe, *Anthills of the Savannah* (London: Heinemann, 1987).
14. Ayi Kwei Armah, *The Healers* (Nairobi: EAPH, 1978).
15. Niyi Osundare, *Village Voices* (Ibadan: Evans Brothers, 1984).
16. Amos Tutuola, *The Palm-wine Drinkard* (London: Faber, 1952).
17. Ama Ata Aidoo, *Anowa* (London: Longman, 1970).
18. Syl Cheney-Coker, *The Last Harmattan of Alusine Dunbar* (London: Heinemann AWS, 1990).
19. Wole Soyinka, *Collected Plays I* (London and New York: OUP, 1973).
20. Wole Soyinka, *Collected Plays II* (London and New York: OUP, 1974).
21. Wole Soyinka, *Death and the King's Horseman* (London: Methuen, 1975).
22. See Oyin Ogunba, 'The Traditional Content of the Plays of Wole Soyinka', *African Literature Today*, 4 (1970).
23. Gabriel Okara, *The Voice* (London: Deutsch, 1964).

24. Ayi Kwei Armah, *The Beautyful Ones Are Not Yet Born* (Boston: Houghton Mifflin, 1968); *Fragments* (Boston: Houghton Mifflin, 1970); *Why Are We So Blest?* (New York: Doubleday, 1972); *Two Thousand Seasons* (Nairobi: EAPH, 1973).
25. Cyprian Ekwensi, *People of the City* (London: Heinemann AWS, 1963; first published London: Dakers, 1954).
26. Ola Rotimi, *The Gods are Not to Blame* (London: Heinemann AWS, 1977).
27. Ngũgĩ wa Thiong'o, *Petals of Blood* (London: Heinemann AWS, 1977).
28. Wole Soyinka, *Season of Anomy* (London: Rex Collings, 1973; New York: Third Press, 1974).

Orality versus Literacy in Mazisi Kunene's *Emperor Shaka the Great*

Wole Ogundele

I Modern African literature right from the beginning has drawn upon two major traditions and their respective thought and imaginative systems: the Western literary tradition and the African oral tradition. One insists on the epistemological difference between history and fiction, the other on the pragmatic identicalness of both. For the majority of African writers, the two traditions exist to be of mutual assistance in the evolution of the new literature in Africa, and the distinction between history and fiction is accepted as valid.

For a small minority, however, the two traditions exist in a state of rivalry, and literature is more or less equated with history. Mazisi Kunene and Okot p'Bitek are the champions of this view; for them, oral literature is superior to written literature in all its ramifications and the earlier the African artist returns to it, the better. Their view represents a brand of cultural autonomy in which literature is the sum-total of history and culture, and yet somehow bears no structural relationship with other spheres of contemporary African experience and awareness.[1]

The matter would have been quite simple if both authors were producing and transmitting their works, and carrying on their anti-literacy campaign, in the performance medium rather than in that of the written text. But this is not so and we, their admiring readers, have to either reconcile their statements with their deeds, or see how such a conflict between medium and message affects their works.

Legitimate, therefore, are such questions as: Can oral noetics and rhetorics pass through the consciousness and process of writing and still remain unchanged? Can literature that is written perform the same functions, and in the same manner, as oral literature? Have writing and/or its cultural by-products not to some extent 'reshaped and restructured' the consciousness of literate and non-literate Africans alike, including that of the champions of orality? These are large theoretical issues which need to be considered while assessing the presence and importance of the oral tradition in the written literature. As Walter J. Ong makes abundantly clear, the technology of orality is a totalising one while that of writing

9

restructures, differentiates, and decontextualises.[2] To refuse to reckon with this and other fundamental differences between orality and literacy is to refuse to acknowledge the reality of the modern world, and to produce only a literature of nostalgia, a literature that is not part of the new social, political and cultural structures being built slowly, painfully, but surely in Africa. The hostile or ambivalent attitude towards writing is understandable. Writing, plus its cultural or intellectual consequences are associated with the West; the same West that plundered and raped Africa of its traditions and cultural values, in the process super-imposing its own intellectual, social and ethical habits on the continent. Writing is therefore associated with this barbaric activity and is to be hated. But to refuse to dissociate the technology from the unfortunate history, and to fail to recognise the irreversibility of the changes set in motion by that encounter, and turn both to advantage, is to court another rape.

By far the most popular success in seeking to neutralise the medium is Okot p'Bitek's song-poetry genre. But despite its many admirable qualities as poetry, it is essentially static and, in the hands of p'Bitek himself, actually suffers a decline in formalistic qualities and intellectual depth between *Song of Lawino* (1966) and *Two Songs* (1971); the reader cannot wish away the feeling that form, content and idiom have become self-repeating. Such a feeling arises precisely because these poems *are* written poems, and it is mostly in that medium that we encounter them.

Such a formalistic standstill was bound to be, for these poems exist in an incongruent, rather than dialectical state with their medium of composition and transmission. Okot p'Bitek and Mazisi Kunene's position is close to, but should not be confused with, the return-to-roots position of Ngũgĩ wa Thiong'o. wa Thiong'o and Kunene for instance share the belief that all African works not produced in African languages are not African literature.[3] For one thing, wa Thiong'o accepts – takes for granted even – the fact of writing. The lumping together of the three may, however, arise because all are cultural autonomists and therefore have politics underlying their literary positions. But this is precisely where the significant difference lies. wa Thiong'o's politics is that of ideological conflicts between classes in both past and present African societies while that of p'Bitek and Kunene is that of ideological harmony, that of Utopia.

This paper is devoted to a formalistic and thematic study of Kunene's *Emperor Shaka the Great*,[4] to show how the informing political affection is utopian. That utopian predisposition is manifested in his often repeated preference for the oral culture over the literate and, as regards the poem itself, in his insistence that his narrative in its entirety is factual even when he proceeds to erect a fictional construct. Indeed, by this valuation of history over fiction, which Kunene finds sufficient support for in Zulu oral tradition, we know that the cultural autonomy he is championing is a specific form of political order. This ideal African political order he finds to have been actualised during Shaka's reign.

II Quite early in his own introduction to the text, Kunene announces his programme and aim as follows:

> ... it is necessary to cut through the thick forest of propaganda and misrepresentation that have been submitted by colonial reports and historians. The following epic poem is an attempt to present an honest view of the achievements of Shaka (p. xiii).

The last ambiguous statement sets up two series of conflicts: between the reports of the outsider (colonial historians) and the oral accounts of the traditional (Zulu) poet-historian; between fact and fiction; and, taken in absolute terms, between the workings of the literate mind and those of the oral mind. All are embodied in Kunene himself who, though a *writer*, wishes to re-immerse himself in the oral tradition but whose very consciousness is that of a twentieth-century literate; culturally, he shares in the outsider status of the coloniser. There is also the conflict between the political ideology of the coloniser and those of the pre-colonised and present African respectively.

This series of conflicts can be streamlined, at the literary level, into that between legend/myth and biography/history, or between the poet and the historian. All of the introduction (complete with lists and genealogies) to the book is meant to persuade us as to the factuality, or at least factual base, of the ensuing narrative, and that this is a corrective biography of Shaka. But the art of biography, as Ira Bruce Nadel has convincingly argued, consists largely in the creative interpretation of facts, in the substitution of one myth (fiction) for another.[5] That is to say, the biographer must primarily be aware that there is a basic, epistemological distinction between fact and fiction before he can make the former serve the latter. And there is also the modern politico-cultural ideology which confines fiction (literature) into the realm of the contemplative and unreal. These go against Kunene's oral poetic which recognises no philosophical distinction between the actual and the imagined, and in which the sole, implicit theory of literature is pragmatism. Thus, his epic narrative of Shaka's life is shot through with infolding paradoxes. It is a literary work in which the poetic of oral tradition rules, but the narrative substructure cannot but be that of the written composition; a biography that has all the features of legend; a fictional narrative that tends towards historiography but nevertheless resolves itself in mythography. It is only by analysing the two main narrative modes of realism and mythism present in the poem that we can find our way through the maze.

Kunene in *Emperor Shaka* has set himself two mutually opposing tasks concerning the presentation of his hero. On the one hand is the need to present Shaka realistically, to situate him and his deeds within the period in which he lived so that he should emerge as a psychologically individuated human being. We should identify with this Shaka because he is a mortal like us. On the other is the public Shaka who must be presented arche-typally, as a symbol of the sum-total of black achievements that are dif-ferent from but equal to those of any other race. But although the mythical Shaka should issue directly out of the realistic one, the two require two different – and not always compatible – narrative modes: the one an inward turn of narrative which gives his character empirical as well as psychological reality and thereby establishes his historical personality; the other an outward turn that, stressing his public actions, establishes his mythical identity and universal blackness. The first mode is modern and very literary, the other ancient and fundamentally oral. We shall examine the operations of these two modes one after the other.

Kunene's reconstruction of Shaka's private life-story avails itself of the modern techniques of characterisation, and the personality that emerges from this is not different from that of the hero of any modern realistic novel. Firstly, he has brought in materials and details of Shaka's life that are more suited to the leisurely pace of the novel but not to the furious pace of the *izibongo*: Shaka's controversial birth and trouble-ridden youth; his later diplomatic handling of the white man's threatening presence; his loneliness and his political struggles to move away from autocracy towards monarchical republicanism. The character of his wars has also been changed from that of mere indulgence in masculine assertiveness to that of political actions necessary for order and unity among the black peoples. Complete with motivations which transform themselves from the initially personal (revenge) to the ultimately impersonal, these materials have been structured together into a logical narrative in which character and event interact to produce a plot of change and development. Kunene relies on modern thoughts on the twin concepts of time and psychology to do this, and to make the all-conquering, nation-building hero continuous with Shaka the rejected child and angry youth.

But these thematic and narrative elements can only lead to the kind of novelistic narrative which distinguishes past from present, and results in extreme individuation of personality and experience. The epic actually at many points moves in this direction, threatening to become merely 'the commemoration of an individual life' (Nadel, p. 105). For instance, Shaka is recurrently presented as a dreamer, a mysterious and lone figure always questioning conventional ideas, overturning customs, and even going as far as to advocate a decisive break with the past in certain areas of social life:

> General, I have always hated the shackles of custom. For, after all, in human affairs there are no eternal laws. Each generation makes a consensus of its own laws. They do not bind for ever those still to be born (Book 4, p. 55)

In other words, there is in Shaka a scepticism born of an awareness of the separateness of past from present, and a potential freedom of individual choice and action. Both are at play in his confrontation with his father (Book 4) and in the generation conflict between him and his adopted father Dingiswayo, over the aims and purposes of war. All these follow the novelistic process of representing an inner and outer life fundamentally at variance with society. If pursued, this line of narrative would have led to imitation of history and therefore satisfy Kunene's aim of presenting an 'honest' (i.e. historically realistic) view of Shaka. But Kunene plays a narrative sleight-of-hand here; as far as tradition is concerned, Shaka is only a purifier who seeks to return society to the original act of the Ancestors. He is different only because outstanding. Hence the philosophical debates that weave in and out of battles and give them meaning by re-affirming a return to the ancestral beginning: 'A new season must be fertilised by old leaves' (Book 3, p. 38). Kunene no doubt also intends these debates to portray a self-reflective political culture, and to show the Shakan era as a historic period when the nation was ruled by a politico-military, home-grown intelligentsia at once sacral and secular, and revolutionary. But these debates and reflections do actually run in proverbs and are resolved in saws and gnomes. For instance, the heated argument between Dingiswayo and Shaka over the latter's new morality of war amounts to no more than the cautious voice of old age checking the tempestuous zeal of youth. Through Kunene's own mastery of traditional oral rhetoric, rather than through the logics of narrative and character developments, an alienated individual of truly revolutionary thoughts is overwhelmed by tradition and deflected into becoming a purifier of culture and mere innovator.

But if the realistic Shaka depends on the fictional technique of verisimilitude for his portrayal rather than on historical verifiability, the other Shaka is even more completely dependent on the age-old motifs of mythical creation. This other Shaka is to be presented as the paradigm of the greatness and regenerative vitality of ancestral values. Shaka is to act in the functional and technical capacity of transmitting tradition through the 'remind and recall' *raison d'être* of oral tradition.[6] And since this tradition is more axiomatic than empirical, any hero who embodies it can only be symbolic, not historical, even if taken from history. Through the non-representational mode of narrative, the emphasis has to be on social and public identity. And although only indirectly evident in the epic, narrative time too has to switch from the historical one of realism to the perpetual one of myth.

III The non-representational mode can be outlined in the most significant aspects of the narrative: in the life of the hero; in the tropes used to present the essence and importance of that life; and in the alternating tragicomic moods of events. Kunene's Shaka is as much a product of the transmutation of experience by imagination as any purely mythical hero. We may outline the events of his life as narrated by Kunene as follows:

(a) Shaka's birth and future greatness prophesied by the diviner.
(b) He is born, a product of a tempestuous, uncontrollable passion and unorthodox union between a prince and a princess.
(c) Mother and child rejected by father who, as king, is afraid and jealous of the foretold greatness of his son. He orders the child's death but the Ancestors prevent it.
(d) The young boy Shaka has a trouble-ridden youth and escapes many dangers; but exile gives his charmed life the bitter experience of loneliness and fosters an uncommon love between mother and son.
(e) Nevertheless, he grows up under a loving foster father to become a young soldier of unusual strength, courage and intelligence, displaying all the promise of his predicted greatness.
(f) Upon the death of his father, chaos ensues at home and he returns a hero and saviour.
(g) He starts his reign as an underdog but soon confounds all his enemies in war after war; builds a formidable army and in the process, the motivation of revenge changes to that of desire for the unity and greatness of the Palm Race (the black peoples).
(h) Public successes are followed and intermittently punctuated by personal sorrows, deaths in the family and a return of the loneliness of his youth and exile days.
(i) Betrayal by a political confidant and assassination at the prime of life.

It is almost superfluous to point out the almost total similarity between this plot pattern and that of the 'Universal Myth' of the hero, as has been documented by Rank, Raglan and Campbell in their separate researches, and summarised by Clyde Kluckhorn.[7] The details omitted in the above outline indeed make the similarities total: the use of dreams and omens and divinations at every crucial turn of events; the great narrative emphasis on the hero's mother who, though not deified upon her death, is mourned as if she had been and appears, god-like, to her son in dreams; and the father-son antagonism which is in binary opposition to the mother-son intimacy. Present in these opposing filial relationships too are the outlines of the Oedipal-type myths which Kluckhorn considers a form of the Hero Myth.[8] One detail of the universal pattern missing in Kunene's narrative is the divine ancestry of the hero. Shaka may have aristocratic and very mortal parents, but throughout it is continually stressed that he is the chosen one, the son of the Ancestors who have endowed him with their own sublime wisdom, knowledge and power. He is in fact not just their chosen one, he is the Ancestors incarnate. He thus combines in his being the mortality and presentness of the living with the mysteriousness and immortality of the 'Beautiful Ones'.

This subsuming of whatever historical kernel Kunene might have used under a mythical pattern is further underlined and amplified by his profuse use of metaphors. The metaphor, Nadel says, represents the power of fiction to redescribe reality; it is a synchronic axis of narrative which intersects the chronological one in that it breaks down the divisions of time and merges past with present. It is essentially an interpretative and evaluative device (Nadel, pp. 159–60).

Three types of imagery are used to describe, interpret and show forth the Shaka essence: animal imagery, especially that of birds and beasts of prey; elemental imagery; and celestial imagery – the sun. The first type is to be expected in a narrative about war and is actually conventional in oral poetry. The elemental images are of two types, those of the destructive elements like fire, whirlwind, thunder-bolt and lightning, and those of mountain, river and vegetation. Not quite different from the animal images, the first sub-type of elemental imagery conveys the irresistible power of Shaka, his elemental nature and the awesome beauty of his army in action. These images too are common in epics. Of the second sub-type, the most recurrent and significant is the mountain symbol. In the poem it has the same meanings as those which Cirlot says man has always symbolised by the mountain: inner loftiness of spirit; greatness and generosity of [Shaka] the emperor; the centre of the [Zulu] world; and the point of contact between heaven and earth (i.e. between the Ancestors and the living generation).[9] But by far the most important symbol in the poem is the sun. Shaka is not only compared to it, he is the sun (pp. 161, 190, 422). Again, Cirlot is relevant here: the sun is the heroic principle at its brightest, the direct son and heir of heaven, 'the active principle and the source of life and energy' (Cirlot, p. 302). Shaka is presented as all these, which attributes the mountain symbol further deepens, magnifies and earths. Just as the sun symbol connects with that of the mountain to stress the theme of Shaka's spiritual sublimity issuing forth in heroic action, so does it link up with that of the lion (the most frequent animal image applied to him) to reiterate his other life-myth as 'the possessor of strength and of the masculine principle', during whose era chivalry is exalted.

But the mythic imagination 'always works from awareness of binary oppositions toward their progressive mediation' (Kluckhorn, p. 63), and so it is in *Emperor Shaka.* There are such oppositions between Shaka and his mother, and within each of them. For instance, the ties that bind mother and son are as delicate and strong by the time of her demise as they were at the beginning; but the two inevitably grow apart once the son's career is under way. The separation becomes a muted conflict on the issue of Shaka's refusal to marry and give her (legitimate) grandchildren. Nandi is the main character in the poem symbolising the complex of female principles: to Senzanghakona (her husband) and her enemies, she is the evil enchantress; to her son, the enduring maternal love and still-point in the whirlwind of wars and court intrigues that are his life, and at the same time the vulnerable part of his life that must be overcome in order for him to follow the true path of his destiny (Book 14, pp. 321–3). Where Shaka is identified with heaven (through the images of mountain, sun and lion), she is the earth – 'the Great Parent from whose breast humanity is fed' (Book 11, p. 268).

Through this image of nourishment, however, the two come together, the oppositions mediated. Thus, her first illness is reported rhetorically: 'The nourishment of our lives has been curtailed by winter' (Book 11, p. 240) and when she dies, she is described as 'the parent who nursed the young' (Book 14, p. 339). Shaka is also the great nourisher of life: he is 'the sun that shines in all regions' and makes 'the tender plants grow beside the tall trees! His wisdom is complemented:

> What you say enriches our lives
> And infuses them with a new sun.
> (Book 12, p. 296)

The binary oppositions are mediated through the motif of nourishment which has existential as well as political and religious dimensions. The Ancestors are of course the great nourishers of all generations. Through their sacrifice, they imbued the present generation with great ideas; Shaka's generation too is doing the same for the future. Together, the two constitute the metaphysical essence and historical identity of the nation, which is in turn the nourisher of every worthy individual. Thus expounds Mghobozi:

> I shall rejoice to die for the nation that I love
> By its power I was nourished from its beginnings
> until I grew tall.
> (Book 12, p. 285)

War is destructive, but death in war is an act of giving back to the nation what it has given in abundance to the heroes, so that the stock of nourishment is never depleted but multiplied.

Amplifying the binary oppositions in the entire epic are the alternate moods of comedy and tragedy: public life and glory alternating with private existence and sorrow; glorification of military heroism set against a longing for peace and domestic tranquillity; a life of action against a meditative one; loneliness against comradeship; loyalty against treachery; fear of death alternating with reconciliation with and anticipation of it; and so on. All these combine to indicate Kunene's effort to make his epic evoke 'a world with a fully open, potentially infinite mimetic horizon,' and this ecumenic character is evident in the narrative movement.[10]

Roughly, the first half of the poem, in a fast narrative pace, deals with the big wars, reaching a climax in the final defeat of Zwide (Book 8). This is the peak of Shaka's military ascendancy and from here the tempo slows down. From Book 9 on, the wars fought are little more than mopping up operations. The major task now is the consolidation of the empire, mostly through the peaceful art of statecraft, but also through occasional battles when necessary. But no sooner does Shaka settle down to this task than the white man makes his destabilising entry into the empire. In Book 11, there is peace, prosperity and general happiness, but all is suddenly counterposed by Nandi's illness. From this moment, there is more talking than fighting, fulfilment and frustration succeed each other regularly and rapidly, and when Shaka's sun reaches its zenith, the cloud of treachery that will overwhelm it begins to form. He is possessed by the desire to cheat death and make his loved ones immortal. But as if to mock him, the dream of Mghobozi's death comes to him. This soon comes to pass on the battlefield, followed by that of his old mentor Mbikwane, and then Nandi's – all interspersed by fleeting moments of victory and celebration. No wonder in one such moment he utters: 'My youth has ended and I am old and wise' (Book 14, p. 325). At her death he says in despair: 'I shall choose my moments of joy in between sadness' (Book 14, p. 336).

From this moment he stops fighting death, reconciles himself to it and now wants an heir; he also begins to anticipate his own death. It could even be said that he invited the assassination by laying himself bare of guards and thereby giving courage to his cowardly half-brothers. Toward the end (Book 16) he in fact sums up his life to his young friend Zihlandlo:

I feel as if I am as old as the Ancestors
But now I dance alone. It is too late.
(Book 16, p. 419)

Whereupon he hands over his favourite spear of many battles as a farewell gift (to posterity). A careful reading of these last pages reveals Kunene's deliberate mythopoeic art: as an 'old man' Shaka is already in touch with the Ancestors (his grandfather Jama); as a dying man he reviews his life and makes the compulsive request to be thought well of after his death; and as an epic hero chosen to bring about the greatness of his people, he is satisfied that he has accomplished his mission. This Shaka is no longer the unique historical individual deserving a commemorative biography, but a prototype found only in the fictional world of myths, epics and tragedies. The neat narrative symmetry of mythical form and design completes the process of fictionalisation.

IV   The end of this fictionalisation of history is of course to create two myths of a symbiotic relationship, a personal 'life-myth' of Shaka and a political myth engendered by the personal one. One is tragic-like, the other comic. In the poem, the mediating agency between the two is the metaphysical-political-social entity called the Ancestors. Brought into the narrative as frequently as Homer brought in the Olympian gods in his own epics, these Ancestors are neither gods, nor a mere epic convention, however. They are simply the illustrious dead. The Ancestors are the mystical life-force which connects the beginning with all succeeding generations, or as Basil Davidson has so picturesquely described them (in another context), the Ancestors are those 'recognised as standing in the line of succession back to the power without beginning'. Their office is to channel this power which enhances life, protects all generations and guarantees the future, to living men.[11] In the poem they constitute a personal guardian spirit for Shaka, precisely because he carries in him that 'power without beginning' which he would use to multiply the greatness of the Palm Race.

The founding of a great nation and empire; the forging of unity based on a common political culture and identification with the emperor; the organisation of an invincible army as midwife to and bulwark of that empire; plus a revolution; all demonstrating a high level of intellectual autonomy and attainment; these are the thematic constituents of the political myth in *Emperor Shaka*. They also constitute a foundation myth calculated to counteract apartheid and its politics of divide-and-oppress, create a single identity among the diverse black ethnic groups, and restore self-confidence and pride in that identity and its historical evolution. It is a nationalistic myth derived as much from ancient sources as from modern ones, foreign and native. One of the possible foreign sources of this foundation-nationalistic myth is worth considering, for it enhances our appreciation of the poem, and the political myth it promotes.

As an epic narrative of a foundation myth, *Emperor Shaka* has much in common with *The Aeneid*. Indeed, so close are the parallels and echoes in narrative movement, characterisation, and the idea of heroism, that one is almost persuaded that Kunene took as much from that Roman poem as from the Zulu *izibongo*. However, influence or congruence, a comparison of the two poems further illuminates the nature of Kunene's own political myth.

As a kind of cultural background, one may note that both poems have behind them the oral epic (Homer) or heroic poem (*izibongo*) which they have to go beyond, functionally and ontologically: their own respective poems have to go beyond the 'remind and recall' function of the oral composition to become acts of creation. The act of creation means giving a novel meaning and emphasis to the heroic outlook, in response to contemporary political needs and cultural valuations. C.M. Bowra has put admirably this original heroic outlook in Virgil:

> Virgil revealed a new field both for glory and for sacrifice. The cause which
> deserves the one and inspires the other was for him not an ideal of individual
> prowess but of service to Rome . . . Virgil abandons the scheme of life by which
> the hero lives and dies for his own glory, and replaces a personal by a social
> ideal.[12]

This completely describes the heroic outlook in *Emperor Shaka*. From this identity issues a series of parallels between Aeneas and Shaka, and their respective experiences. Like Aeneas, Kunene's Shaka is the man appointed by destiny (here, the Ancestors) to found a nation, a task before which all other considerations (most especially private, sexual love and a settled family life) must give way. Shaka is also the superlative warrior and strategist who nevertheless feels more keenly the tragedy of war than its exhilarating glory, and therefore fights more out of necessity than love of this aristocratic occupation.

In both characters resides an abiding, soft nature which counters their warrior temper and steely resolution. (In the case of Shaka, this sentimental nature makes him a perpetually vulnerable individual and leader.) One may also mention that both are given to 'outbursts of anger and fury' (Bowra, p. 67) as well as great grief, but are gradually brought by sad experiences into the stoic state of equanimity and wisdom, deepened, in Shaka's case, by the mystical aspect of his nature. The comparison may be rounded off by placing Kunene's definition of the Zulu heroic ideal side by side with the ideal of Roman virtue which Aeneas embodies. The Zulu communal organisation, Kunene says, is anchored in the belief 'that the highest virtue is not justice . . . but heroism, that is, self-sacrifice on behalf of the community.'[13] This is identical with the Roman Virtue which, as put by Donald Earl, 'consisted in the winning of personal pre-eminence and glory by the commission of great deeds in the service of the Roman state'[14] Or, as stated by Cicero, glory is 'praise given to right action and the reputation for great merits in the service of the republic . . .'[15] This is the ideal by which Shaka and his generals prosecuted their wars and on which they endeavoured to found the new empire. For them, it means doing one's duty by the Ancestors, the nation, and the future generations.

Of the multiple incidents that give substance to this ideal, only three need be cited. Shaka on the threshold of his career explains to his mother why he cannot marry:

> But then my failure to give is not of my doing.
> It is the task given to me by my forefathers
> To enhance the name of their ancient nation.
> (Book 5, p. 103)

He must postpone domestic joys; moreover, procreation weakens the body and, later in life, a king begins to fear death 'for his children's sake'. Again, there are Mbikwane's last words to the effect that he is happy to die because he has fulfilled the task given to him by the nation and the Ancestors (Book 12, p. 294). Lastly, Mghobozi's life is one entirely consecrated to this ideal, which his death too seals:

> I shall be glad to die in the battlefield.
> I shall rejoice to die for the nation that I love

By its power I was nourished from its beginnings until
I grew tall.
(Book 12, p. 285)

This Zulu version of the Roman *pietas* – for which the semi-abstract meta-phor is nourishment – is what Kunene perceives as the ancestral founda-tion on which Shaka successfully built the Zulu empire. A political behaviour wrapped in an ethical order, it is the chief thematic focus of the foundation myth which the poet wishes to revive through the re-creation of the Shaka life-story.

But foundation myths, as Henry Tudor argues, 'explain the present in terms of a creative act that took place in the past'. The act may be an ancient legend, 'but in most cases', Tudor goes on, 'it is an actual and often quite recent historical event which has been dramatised for the purpose of a political argument' (Tudor, p. 91). A foundation myth should thus be a success story. But if the rise of Shaka and his building of an empire are a success story, not so the subsequent events in South Africa, starting with the assassination of Shaka himself. Kunene's foundation myth, in terms of a reconstructed past, neither leads up to nor explains the present. It stops precisely at that moment when the momentous events that inaugurated the present began.

The gap between past and present in the narrative does reveal, how-ever, the true nature of the myth Kunene has created: a nationalist myth, manifesting the ideology of cultural authenticity and self-sufficiency; nostalgia for an imagined unified past complete with a single set of Ancestor-heroes; and a single political ethics for all the black groups in South Africa. Thus the qualifier 'Zulu' in the subtitle is meant to differen-tiate the poem's Africanness from the Western epic tradition. The poem is to be a national epic – *à la Virgil* – for the 'black nation' in South Africa. Relevant here is one of the underlying tenets of the doctrine of nationalism: that every nation 'is defined by its past and therefore must have a past to be defined by . . .'[16] From it springs the mythologisation of history so that every past is national and all past achievements expressions of the 'national' genius, to be commemorated, preserved, 'and revived because they establish "national" identity and foster pride in it' (Kedourie, p. 64). Since the element of pride presupposes that the reconstruction of the past must stress victories and gloss over defeats, it follows that the events inaugurating the unhappy present must suffer narrative structural amnesia. History then becomes not an inductive process by which a total account of as much of the past as is recoverable is arrived at, but a selective emphasising of the high peaks of achievement. In this light, what Kunene corrects and rewrites is not history but an hegemonic tradition.

Thus the kind of political ideology explicitly promoted by this revised tradition: the heroic epithets attached to Shaka and other heroes; the metaphor of nourishment; the doctrine of the Ancestors; all resurrect a political order based on an uncritical attachment to the nation as incarnated in its leader(s) who are 'innately' superior to the led. To these leaders the subjects are related solely by ties of dependency (Kedourie, p. 25). As narrated in the poem, the responses to Nandi's and Shaka's deaths are the most undisguised statements of this ideology. The point about these part-ritualised, part-anarchic responses is that they portray these deaths as personal losses suffered by every subject in the kingdom, and hence constitute the 'pathetic fallacy' aspect of the myth of nationalism; that is, an emotional link of love 'between leader and led in which the leader satisfies to satiety his will to power and the led, in turn, feel at one with their master.' This fallacy safeguards the belief that the interests, preoccupations and aims of both are 'exactly identical' (Kedourie, p. 131). In the poem, this exact identity is stressed at every point, even by the portrayal of the dissenters. Although supported by Princess Mkhabayi, Shaka's half-brothers do not oppose him openly because they have nothing to oppose him with except petty grudges and envy. Instead, their conspiracy is portrayed as indicating their lack of nourishment from the Ancestors.

In resurrecting this ancient political order, however, Kunene gives it a touch of modernity by bringing to it the millennial aspects of revolutionary nationalism. The 'pursuit of the millennium' has no room for opposition and this, above any dramatic weakness in the poem, explains Shaka's godlike superiority over every other character, and why his half-brothers are reduced to mere disgruntled and grumbling cretins. With this technical elimination of any worthwhile internal opposition, Shaka is given a completely free hand to concentrate on actualising his vision of the millennium.

In Book 14, that millennium is in place and the narrative resumes with the line: 'The king was exuberant with life'. The king's good health and happiness are the nation's. There then follows a detailed account of different sorts of lively sports, rounded off with a description of the nation enjoying an idyllic state, personified again in Shaka:

> After this event huge fires were lit to roast meat.
> A season of plenty and fun dominated throughout Zulu land.
> . . . .
> Women wore their chosen feathers of birds of paradise,
> Blending the beauty of their adornments with those of the king.
> He was tall and splendid in his white and green epaulettes of beads
> (Book 14, p. 321)

Shaka's military reorganisations and political and social reforms were set in motion towards the achievement of this perfect state. He is a magical personality who will return in another 'fifteen decades', for he is as eternal as the comet (Book 17, p. 422) or, like the Ancestors who are forever returning because 'they were here at the beginning of time'. In the closing oracular dirge, Shaka is resurrected and apotheosised as a nature divinity

(p. 433). 'Even now they sing his song. They call his name.' Thus does Kunene transmute biography into legend, legend into a religious myth, and that myth into a political cult. Thus, too, does the quest for cultural authenticity, via the route of oral tradition – which Kunene talks about in more theological than historical or aesthetic terms – lead to a retrospective discovery of the political doctrine of divine monarchy, being recommended implicitly for adoption now.

VI Kunene's Shaka (and the entire poem, too) belongs to the phase of political nationalism in Africa – the period of intense romanticisation of the past. That period continued into roughly the first decade after independence when nationalists who had become heads of modern republics attempted to sacralise and personalise authority under the guise of national integration. It is interesting how much Kunene's Shaka corresponds with the mystique of the semi-divine monarch that several post-independence African leaders tried to build around themselves. As itemised and analysed by Ali A. Mazrui, this process of political mystification and personality-cult building combined at least four elements of political style: the quest for aristocratic effect; the personalisation of authority; the sacralisation of authority; and the quest for a royal historical identity.[17] (Kunene did not of course have to fabricate the last element for Shaka.) Mazrui in the same article also talks of the attempt by these leaders – and the nation which they saw themselves as embodiments of – to be traditional and modern at the same time. It was not a case of modernising tradition, but of fossilising and exhibiting it as evidence of past greatness. In the event, cultural schizophrenia led to regression in political culture.

One can discern a roughly parallel development in Kunene's poem. According to Kunene himself, the subject of the poem had been in his mind while in high school,[18] and K.L. Goodwin tells us that he (Kunene) started working on it from the early 1960s,[19] both periods coincide, respectively, with that of private romantic outlook and that of collective (African) romanticisation of the past. Oral tradition is the synecdoche of that idealised past and should therefore be retained at all cost; writing is that of the present and should be rejected at all cost. Thus, although *Emperor Shaka* is a written poem, the overarching modes of thought and imagination that shaped it are oral. In the making of the poem itself, romantic outlook has hardened into utopian mentality which, as defined by Karl Mannheim, occurs when a state of mind 'is incongruous with the reality within which it occurs'. 'This incongruence', Mannheim explains further, 'is always evident in the fact that such a state of mind in experience, thought, and in practice, is oriented towards objects which do not exist in the actual situation.'[20] Fiction is an empire which, when denied, strikes back in unexpected ways.

NOTES

1. Okot p'Bitek, *Africa's Cultural Revolution* (Nairobi: Macmillan Books for Africa, 1973) chs. 3-5. Kunene, interview with Jane Wilkinson, *Commonwealth: Essays and Studies*, 10.2 (Spring 1988): 34-42.
2. Compare Walter J. Ong's discussion with p'Bitek's assertion that 'Now words can be spoken, sung or written. The voice of the singer or the speaker and the pen and paper are mere midwives of a pregnant mind. A song is a song whether it is sung, spoken or written down', p'Bitek: 20. I am indebted to Ong's *Orality and Literacy: The Technologization of the Word* (London: Methuen, 1982) in this part of the essay.
3. See Ngũgĩ wa Thiong'o, *Writers in Politics* (London: Heinemann, 1981): 53-9 where he calls 'Afro-European Literature', all African writings produced in European languages; and Kunene, 'The Relevance of African Cosmological Systems to African Literature Today', *African Literature Today*, 11 (1980): 190-205.
4. Mazisi Kunene, *Emperor Shaka the Great: A Zulu Epic* (London: Heinemann, 1979).
5. Ira Bruce Nadel, *Biography: Fiction, Fact and Form* (London: Macmillan, 1984): ch. 5.
6. Eric A. Havelock, *Preface to Plato* (Cambridge Mass.: Harvard University Press, 1963): 91.
7. Clyde Kluckhorn, 'Recurrent Themes in Myths and Mythmaking', *The Making of Myth*, ed. Richard M. Ohmann (New York: G.P. Putnam Sons, 1962): 52-65.
8. Kluckhorn: 61. For a brief discussion of the Oedipal myth in *Emperor Shaka*, see John Haynes, *African Poetry and the English Language* (London: Macmillan, 1985): ch. 5.
9. J.E. Cirlot, *A Dictionary of Symbols*, transl.: Jack Sage (London: Routledge & Kegan Paul, 1962): 208-9.
10. Paul Hernadi, *Beyond Genre: New Directions in Literary Classification* (Ithaca: Cornell University Press, 1972): 181-2.
11. Basil Davidson, *The Africans: An Entry to Cultural History* (Middlesex: Penguin Books, 1973): 49.
12. C.M. Bowra, *From Virgil to Milton* (London: Macmillan, 1963): 13.
13. Mazisi Kunene, *Zulu Poems* (New York: Africana Pub. Corp., 1970): 11.
14. Quoted in Henry Tudor, *Political Myth* (London: Pall Mall Press, 1972): 24.
15. Tudor: 75.
16. Elie Kedourie, ed., *Nationalism in Asia and Africa* (London: Frank Cass & Co., 1971): 92.
17. Ali A. Mazrui, 'The Monarchical Tendency in African Political Culture', reproduced in *Violence and Thought: Essays on Social Tensions in Africa* (London: Longmans, Green & Co., 1969): 206-7.
18. *Commonwealth*, 10.2 (Spring 1988): 37.
19. K.L. Goodwin, *Understanding African Poetry: A Study of Ten African Poets* (London: Heinemann, 1982): 173.
20. Karl Mannheim, *Ideology and Utopia: An Introduction to the Sociology of Knowledge* (London: Routledge & Kegan Paul, 1963): 173.

Oral Traditions & Modern Poetry: Okot p'Bitek's *Song of Lawino* & Okigbo's *Labyrinths*

Charles A. Bodunde

The African writer must first look back to his own heritage. Then he must look around at what is available to him. If he decides to adapt existing forms to suit his needs, he can still bring to those forms trends of identity and distinction which will give him a place in the forms known and accepted by the world at large.

Cyprian Ekwensi[1]

Introduction

In his 'Oral Tradition and the Contemporary Theatre in Nigeria' Joel Adedeji provides a working definition of oral tradition which details the purpose and mode of acquiring this verbal act. He suggests that oral tradition is the 'complex corpus of verbal or spoken art created as a means of recalling the past'. For him, it is 'based on the ideas, beliefs, symbols, assumptions, attitude and sentiments of peoples' and the mode of acquisition is 'through a process of learning or initiation and its purpose is to condition social action and foster social interaction'.[2] The typology of oral tradition enumerated by Adedeji recognises two main categories, namely, literary and historical.[3] In his classification, the literary category includes poetic genres such as *oriki* or praise and totem chants, *odu* or Ifa divination poems and songs. The literary category also includes formulae like proverbs, parables and incantations. The historical category includes such forms as narratives based on myths, legends and historical lays like the epic. A similar classification is made by Harold Scheub in his article 'Review of African Oral Traditions and Literature', where he gives the major divisions of oral traditions as 'the riddle and lyric poems; the proverb; and the tale, heroic poetry and epic.'[4]

One of the characteristics of oral tradition which relates to the nature of performance is the involvement of the community in the creative process as well as in the criticism. For instance, Finnegan reveals that in a creative performance, members of the audience neither listen silently nor wait for the chief performer's invitation to join in. Instead, the audience

24

break into the performance with their additions, questions and criticism.[5] A further evidence of communal involvement in the creation of the verbal art is provided by Macebuh. He maintains that 'the farmer, the hunter, and the wine-tapper could be relied upon to muster a sufficiently meaningful response to art.' They do this 'as part of their general awareness as citizens of a community of beings'.[6]

The influence which the various elements of oral traditions exert on modern African writing especially poetry, is indeed tremendous. In fact, major African literary texts indicate attachment to the African cosmic setting. This is the setting which Mazisi Kunene describes as the primary basis of all literatures.[7] Part of the reason why many African writers borrow from the stock of oral traditions can be attributed to the writers' recognition of the functions which verbal art forms perform in the society. For instance, William Bascom believes that verbal art forms such as myths and legends 'contain detailed descriptions of sacred ritual, the codified belief or dogma of the religious system of the people'.[8] A.H. Gayton amplifies this idea in his 'Perspectives in Folklore' when he argues that the mythological system of a people is often their educational system and that the children who sit listening to an evening's tale under the bright moonlight are imbibing traditional knowledge and attitudes.[9] In a study of education among the Chaga of East Africa, Raum also observes that the intrinsic value of proverbs to the people lies in two qualities. They are regarded as 'inheritance from their ancestors incorporating the experience of the tribe, and they serve as instruments both for self control and for the control of others'.[10]

Both Okot p'Bitek and Christopher Okigbo are significantly influenced by African oral traditions. Like other African artists, they borrow from the rich African verbal art forms to create new visions of life and new poetic idioms with remarkable originality. These borrowings occur in the form of imaginative use of African traditional symbols, images, proverbs, myths and other traditional stylistic devices.

Okot p'Bitek's *Song of Lawino*

Symbols

Adrian Roscoe's comment on *Song of Lawino* in his *Uhuru's Fire* touches on Okot p'Bitek's imaginative use of oral traditions. Roscoe declares that Okot p'Bitek's song 'has been a truly seminal development' and that its success 'stems in part from its relationship to oral tradition'. He emphasises that Okot p'Bitek's achievement is that, 'better than most African poets, he has created in *Song of Lawino* a form which is popular and the outgrowth of home tradition'.[11] One of the conspicuous traditional icons in Okot p'Bitek's poetry is symbolism. Lawino, the speaker of the poem relies on the traditional Acholi symbols of the horn, the bull and the spear to lament her husband's loss of traditional qualities.

Among the Acholi, the horn is not only a musical instrument but also a ritual object connected with the initiation into adulthood. In ceremonies, young men blow their horns as signals of their individuality and reputation. Thus, Lawino speaks of her own fame that spreads far beyond her immediate environment like the horn that extends a young man's fame:

> I was the leader of the girls
> And my name blew like a horn
> Among the Payira and I played
> On my bow harp and praised my love.[12]

In her comment on modern day elections, Lawino also uses the horn symbol for effect. She talks of the 'horn loud and proud' of the victorious in contrast to the silent horn of the defeated.

Also among the Acholi, the bull is a panegyric title used as a compliment for bravery and respect. Lawino combines the symbols of the bull and the horn to remind Ocol, her husband, of the respectable and famous ancestry from which he descends. She indicts Ocol for behaving like 'a dog of the white man' (p. 116) and reminds him of his proud ancestry:

> Your grandfather was a Bull among men
> And although he died long ago
> His name still blows like a horn
> His name is still heard
> Throughout the land (p. 116)

Like the horn, the spear possesses a ritual essence. A man is never buried without his spear carefully placed by his side. The phallic significance of the spear is obvious. It is a symbol of masculinity which Lawino uses to capture Ocol's impotence and alienation from tradition:

> When you have gained your full strength
> Go to the shrine of your father,
> Prepare a feast . . .
> Beg forgiveness from them
> And ask them to give you a new spear
> A new spear with a sharp and hard point
> A spear that will crack the rock
> Ask for a spear that you will thrust . . .
> Ask them to restore your manhood!
> For I am sick of sharing a bed with a woman (p. 119)

With the spear symbol, Okot p'Bitek makes a major statement about the effect of modernisation. He warns that too much modernisation paralyses the traditional essence and emasculates victims like Ocol.

Images, Proverbs and Myths

In an introduction to Okot p'Bitek's *Song of Lawino* and *Song of Ocol,*
Heron makes an important statement which underscores the uniqueness
of Okot p'Bitek's use of traditional imagery:

> The most important influence Acholi songs have on *Song of Lawino* is the
> imagery Okot uses. Okot has completely avoided the stock of common images of
> English literature through his familiarity with the stock of common images of
> Acholi literature. (p. 7)

Heron stresses that in the English version, the stock of Acholi imagery
'gives his poem a feeling of freshness for every reader, and a sense of
Africanness for African readers' (p. 7).

Lawino relies on a string of traditional images to criticise Clementina,
her rival for Ocol. She describes the woman's lips as 'red-hot like glowing
charcoal' (p. 37) and when she 'dusts powder on her face, she resembles
the wizard getting ready for the midnight dance' (p. 37). This frightening
image is an appropriate picture that captures the weird adornment that
shows on Clementina's face.

Section eleven of *Song of Lawino* presents independence in the image
of a fallen buffalo which the eager politicians, like hunters rush to
share:

> Independence falls like a bull buffalo
> And the hunters rush to it with drawn knives
> Sharp shining knives for carving the carcass
> And if your chest is small, bony and weak
> They push you off, and if your knife is blunt
> You get the dung on your elbow,
> You come home empty handed
> And the dogs bark at you! (p. 107)

In the same section of the poem, Lawino exposes the poverty and neglect
which the voters are forced to bear after each election. The politicians
'who have fallen into things', throw themselves 'into soft beds while the
hip bones of the voters grow painful sleeping on the same earth they slept
before Uhuru!' (p. 110). She castigates the politicians who abandon the
voters and are rarely seen again after their election victory. Like the local
python 'with a bull water buck in its tummy' (p. 110), the politicians 'hiber-
nate and stay away and eat!' Lawino takes the image of the kite from
Acholi oral song and adapts it to convey the exploitative attitude of the
modern day African politicians who 'return to the countryside for the next
election/like the kite/That returns during the Dry Season' (p. 110).

Proverbs are common features of oral traditions. In *Song of Lawino*, the
central proverb is the one built on the pumpkin. In the Acholi oral tradition, the pumpkin planted around the homestead is never uprooted even
when the old homestead is to be abandoned. The proverb, 'The pumpkin

in the old homestead/must not be uprooted' recurs in the poem. Each time Lawino uses the proverb, it serves as a subtle warning to Ocol who has not only embraced the new way of life brought by modernisation but is set to destroy the old, represented by 'the pumpkin in the old homestead'. Apart from proverbs, Okot p'Bitek uses local sayings to add freshness and weight to his poetry. When Lawino points to the need for an African to be himself, she draws out the picture by using a witty local saying:

> No leopard
> would change into a hyena
> And the crested crane
> would hate to be changed
> Into the bald-headed
> Dung eating vulture
> The long-necked and graceful giraffe
> Cannot become a monkey (p. 56)

One of the technical devices used by Okot p'Bitek in *Song of Lawino* is the incorporation of the Acholi myth to shape Lawino's character as well as the setting of the poem. Unable to understand the process by which electricity works, Lawino falls back to the myth surrounding it in her tradition:

> They say
> When the Rain-cock
> Opens its wings
> The blinding light
> And the deadly fire
> Flow through the wires
> And lighten the streets
> And the houses
> And the fire
> goes into the electric stove (p. 57)

By making Lawino speak this way, Okot p'Bitek sets her and Ocol further apart as characters who belong to different worldviews. Although he may laugh at her for her ignorance, his uprooted state, resulting from the alienating cult of modernity is the more pathetic.

Repetition and Audience Involvement

In *Song of Lawino*, certain phrases are repeated as in the oral performance. The repetition of 'Let no one uproot the pumpkin' throughout the sections of *Song of Lawino* is intended to emphasise Lawino's attempt to preserve traditional values in the face of the destructive enchroachment of Western tradition. Ocol receives verbal lashings from Lawino for his slavish attachment to the white man's social codes. In a biting criticism of the relationship between Ocol and Clementina, Lawino repeats the line 'As white people do' to emphasise Ocol's obsession with the white man's social values:

You kiss her on the cheek
As white people do,
You kiss her open sore lips
As white people do
You suck the slimy saliva
From each other's mouths
As white people do (p. 44)

Audience involvement is a significant aspect of the oral art. Abu Abarry
states that this is so important that its removal will render any oral performance meaningless.[13] Lawino's eagerness to involve the audience in her
narration is signalled by expressions like 'come brother' and 'my
clansmen'. Their use in the poem shows the symbiotic interaction between
the oral performer and the audience. Also, it portrays the fundamental
spirit of collective production that prevails in the African creative arts.

Christopher Okigbo's *Path of Thunder*

Symbols and Images

Although Okigbo is extensively influenced by European poets, there is sufficient evidence of traditional materials in his poetry. Even the 'Troika',
Chinweizu, Jemie and Madubuike, who criticise him along with other poets
for glorifying in 'obscurantism and senseless narcissism' in his earlier
poems, acknowledge his use of oral traditions in 'Path of Thunder':

> The high peak attained by Okigbo in 'Path of Thunder' towers above the low
> irregular landscape of Nigerian poetry in English. So far, the only other peak
> that rivals it in African poetry in English is Okot p'Bitek's *Song of Lawino* which
> is possibly the best rounded single work of African poetry in English today.[14]

The rituals and sacrifices in 'Lustra' are heightened through skilful
association of images and symbols. In this section of *Labyrinths*,[15] the
poet, who has been alienated from the indigenous culture now comes back
like a prodigal wishing to be readmitted into communion with the goddess,
Idoto. The significance of the ritual offering on the part of the poet-hero
is stressed by Dan Izevbaye. He notes that since the poet is technically a
stranger, he requires ritual cleansing. The three parts of 'Lustra' are
therefore concerned with this traditional feast of purification. The 'traditionally prescribed objects of purification' like vegetable offerings, chalk,
long-drums and cannons are ritual symbols intended to effect the poet's
ascent towards acceptance.[16] In the rest of *Labyrinths*, images and symbols such as 'palm-grove,' 'weaver-bird', 'the town crier', 'the hornbill'
and 'the sacrificial ram', are used for the exploration of the poet's socio-
spiritual state as he searches for purification, acceptance into the traditional culture and poetic illumination.

Traditional Poetic Forms

Okigbo borrows the invocational and incantatory devices from the oral traditions and uses them imaginatively to draw attention to the traditional religion from which he has been exiled and to which he now returns like a prodigal. In Okigbo's *Labyrinths*, the scenes of sacrifice are occasions for the presentation of the invocational and incantatory tones. This indigenous influence is noted by Egudu who affirms that Okigbo's adaptation of the tone of incantation for his ritual scenes in *Labyrinths* is consistent with the use in which this traditional icon is put 'by every Igbo high priest of the indigenous god'.[17]

Sometimes, Okigbo makes an innovative combination of the incantatory and invocational techniques and the traditional praise-poem. For instance, in 'Siren Limits', he invokes the goddess of the palm groves reflecting the structure of the traditional praise poem:

> Queen of the damp half light,
> I have had my cleansing,
> Emigrant with air-borne nose,
> The he-goat-on-heat. (p. 23)

The traditional praise poem influences the second stanza of Okigbo's 'Hurrah for Thunder'. Here, he describes the might of the elephant, a symbol for the Federal Government during the first regime in Nigeria:

> The elephant, tetrarch of the jungle:
> With a wave of the hand
> He could pull four trees to the ground;
> His four mortar legs pounded the earth:
> Wherever they treaded,
> The grass was forbidden to be there. (p. 67)

The description of the qualities of the elephant echoes the traditional chants (especially the Yoruba *Ijala*) on this animal by the oral artists. S.A. Babalola recognises verbal salute to particular animals as one of the dominant subjects of the Ijala praise poetry. He stresses that the oral artist does this by giving

> a character sketch of the said animal or bird. Such a chant contains information about the physical appearance, the characteristic cry, the characteristic gait and the characteristic habits of the animal or bird.[18]

Some of the animals identified as subjects of this species of traditional poetry are the elephant, the buffalo, the lion and the baboon. Okigbo's 'Hurrah for Thunder' is an imaginative transfer of this local poetic kind into modern poetry. The imaginative use of the praise form allows for an equally imaginative political interpretation. The elephant becomes a symbol of the Federal Government of Nigeria in the sixties which threatened to destroy the four regions of Nigeria (the 'four mortar legs') 'with a wave of the hand'. The destructive brute force of the Government is further underscored by the image of an elephant pulling 'four trees to the ground'.

Proverbs, Repetitions and Musical Accompaniments

Okigbo's *Labyrinths* contains proverbs which are borrowed from oral traditions and modified to suit the socio-political vision intended in the poetry. Helen Chukwuma stresses the importance of proverbs especially when they are borrowed and modified to project opinions in modern African writing:

> Proverbs are used to express an essential idea. When they are used in verse, they are not usually subject to a rendition in their original forms. Rather they are modified and adapted according to the demand of rhythm and beat. Adaptation may take the form of adding a few words or or of contrasting the proverb words while still retaining the essential image necessary for its identification.[19]

Again in 'Hurrah for Thunder' Okigbo hears the hunters, the military, 'already . . . talking about pumpkins' (p. 67). He uses local proverbs to bear the weight of his warning: 'The eye that looks down will surely see the nose' and 'The finger that fits should be used to pick the nose' (p. 67). The two proverbs are direct translations from the local stock of proverbs. The former is strikingly close to the type used by Agboreko in Wole Soyinka's *A Dance of the Forests*:

OLD MAN: Yes, yes, we'll be patient.
AGBOREKO: The eye that looks downwards will certainly see the nose.[20]

What Okigbo intends to communicate through this proverb is similar to Agboreko's amplification of Old Man's plea for patience. Okigbo uses the proverb to caution those in the vanguard of Nigerian politics especially at a crucial moment of the political history of the country.

Like Okot p'Bitek, Okigbo uses repetition as a rhetorical device. Again, Helen Chukwuma locates repetition as 'a basic principle of oral art and can be viewed as a stylistic and fundamental grammatical form'. She offers that 'verbal repetition in oral art is sometimes used as a way of establishing emphasis' and that 'in a typical oral verse, repetition entails not only the structure but the words of the stanzas themselves'.[21] The device of repetition contributes immensely to the music of Okigbo's poetry. In 'Elegy for Slit-drum' where the traditional dirge form is used, repetition helps to intensify the aura of grief as well as the sense of instability that befalls the nation. The word 'condolences' is repeated several times in this section of the poem. Also, some lines are repeated to evoke the elevated sound effect suitable for the dirge form. The following lines are examples:

> the panther has delivered a hare
> the hare is beginning to leap
> the panther has delivered a hare
> the panther is about to leap. (p. 68)

And:

> the elephant has fallen
> the mortars have won the day
> the elephant has fallen
> does he deserve his fate
> the elephant has fallen
> can we remember the date. (p. 67)

Another form of repetition which enhances the musical quality of Okigbo's verse is parallelism. This type not only creates melody, it intensifies the emotional impact which the poet intends to register. One example of such parallelism is the couplet that ends 'Elegy for Slit-drum':

> trunk of the iron tree we cry *condolences* when we break,
> shells of the open sea we cry *condolences* when we shake . . . (p. 70)

And in 'Distances VI', we have another example:

> I have fed out of the drum
> I have drunk out of the cymbal (p. 60)

Ulli Beier, one of the foremost collectors of verbal art forms in Nigeria was so much charmed by the melody of Okigbo's poetry that he commented enthusiastically:

> Everything he touches vibrates and swings and we are compelled to read on and to follow the tune of his chant, hardly worried about the fact that we understand little of what he has to say.[22]

Okigbo uses drum and rattles accompaniments in 'Elegy for Alto' and 'Elegy for Slit-drum' respectively. This is consistent with the use of such musical objects as hollow-wood, resonated pot and rattles in oral performances where poetry is realised in song.[23] There is no doubt that Okigbo shows his originality in the fashioning of new poetic techniques from oral traditions and uses musical accompaniments to create an intensely resonant poetry. His skill in the imaginative use of oral art forms is celebrated by many of the poets who lament his death in *Don't Let Him Die*.[24]

Conclusion

The poetry of Okot p'Bitek and Okigbo reflects the influences which oral traditions exert on modern African poetry. These borrowed materials have the capacity to improve the content and form of modern poetry as indicated in the works of the two poets. Although the modern African poet does not see himself using exactly the same methods of composition as the traditional artist, as Echeruo observes,[25] the echoes of traditional symbols, images and local idioms are enough to create a new poetic style quite distinguishable from the species produced by Western poets. It is a fact that those materials that are borrowed from oral traditions are often expressed in languages that are non-African. However, experienced poets like Okot p'Bitek and Okigbo even in their use of the English language still manage to deploy local symbols, images and traditional poetic devices in such a way as to resonate the artistic experience of the African people with almost as much concern and enthusiasm as the indigenous artists. This is one of the worthy legacies left behind by these two poets.

NOTES

1. Cyprian Ekwensi, 'The Dilemma of the African Writer', *West African Review*, 27 (1956): 701–2.
2. Joel Adedeji, 'Oral Tradition and the Contemporary Theatre in Nigeria', *Research in African Literatures*, 2, 2 (1971): 134.
3. Adedeji: 136.
4. Harold Scheub, 'Review of African Oral Traditions and Literature', *The African Studies Review*, 28, 2/3 (June/September, 1985).
5. Ruth Finnegan, *Oral Literature in Africa* (Oxford: Clarendon Press, 1970): 10–11.
6. S. Macebuh, 'African Aesthetics in Traditional African Art', *Okike*, 5 (1974): 22.
7. See Mazisi Kunene, 'The Relevance of African Cosmological Systems to African Literature Today', *African Literature Today*, 11 (1980): 200.
8. William Bascom, 'Four Functions of Folklore', *Journal of American Folklore*, 67, 226 (1954): 345.
9. A.H. Gayton, 'Perspectives in Folklore', *Journal of American Folklore*, 64 (1951): 149.
10. O.F. Raum, *Chaga Childhood: A Description of Indigenous Education in an East African Tribe* (London: OUP, 1940): 214.
11. Adrian Roscoe, *Uhuru's Fire* (London: Cambridge University Press, 1977): 56.
12. Okot p'Bitek, *Song of Lawino and Song of Ocol* (London: Heinemann, 1984): 48. All subsequent page references are made to this edition and appear in the text.
13. Abu Abarry, 'Oral Rhetoric and Poetics', in *Comparative Approaches to Modern African Literature*, ed. S.O. Asein (Ibadan: Ibadan University Press, 1984): 24.

14. Chinweizu *et al, Toward the Decolonization of African Literature* (Enugu: Fourth Dimension, 1980): 187.
15. Christopher Okigbo, *Labyrinths* (London: Heinemann, 1971). Unless otherwise stated, page references are made to this edition and occur in the text.
16. Dan Izevbaye, 'Okigbo's Portrait of the Artist as a Sunbird: A Reading of *Heavensgate*', *African Literature Today*, 6 (1973): 20.
17. Romanus Egudu, 'Defence of Culture in the Poetry of Christopher Okigbo', *African Literature Today*, 6 (1973): 10.
18. S.A. Babalola, *The Content and Form of Yoruba Ijala* (London: Oxford University Press, 1966): 11.
19. Helen Chukwuma, 'The Oral Nature of Traditional Poetry and Language', *Journal of the Nigerian English Studies*, 8, 1 (May 1976): 17.
20. Wole Soyinka, *A Dance of the Forests* (Oxford: Oxford University Press, 1963): 38.
21. Helen Chukwuma: 16.
22. Ulli Beier, 'Reactions to "Siren Limits" ', *Black Orpheus, 12* (1963) 46–7.
23. Chukwuma: 14.
24. Achebe and Dubem Okafor, eds., *Don't Let Him Die* (Enugu: Fourth Dimension Publishers, 1978).
25. M.J. Echeruo, 'Traditional and Borrowed Elements in Nigerian Poetry', *Nigerian Magazine, 89* (June 1966): 142.

Kofi Awoonor as a Poet

Isaac I. Elimimian

Kofi Awoonor has certain things in common with those African poets I would consider as the traditionalists, particularly Christopher Okigbo, Gabriel Okara, and Okot p'Bitek. Like these poets, he is committed to his cultural roots; like them he treats the conflict of cultures; and like these poets too, he has a strong desire to salvage the indigenous culture from the brutalities of Western colonialism.

Born in 1935 at Wheta in the Volta Region of Ghana, and educated at the Universities of Ghana, London, and the State University of New York, he had a Sierra Leonean father and a Togolese mother. Kofi Awoonor was formerly known as George Awoonor Williams (before he changed his name, apparently because of his disdain for the imported culture).

On account of the above fact, and in view of the zeal and seriousness with which he relishes anything indigenous, one can say that the theme of the celebration of cultural heritage has a special place in his poetry. Awoonor is well versed in his traditional Ewe lore and folk songs, all of which feature prominently in his work. He confesses: 'The translations from which I worked at the earliest period were unpolished and retain a crudity which reflects not only an incomplete grasp of the English Language, but . . . an ineffective rendering of typically Ewe Idioms into English.'[1]

Perhaps because of Awoonor's ability to weave diverse images around a distinctly African experience, Ken Goodwin describes him as a 'syncretist', more so as 'Africa for him is a continent and a notion that draws into itself, appropriating and adapting, the whole human life and history.'[2]

Awoonor's poems which dwell on the theme of cultural heritage include 'More Messages', 'Songs of Sorrow', 'My Uncle the Diviner-Chieftain', and 'A Dirge'. 'More Messages' deals with the predicament of the poet who is bent on celebrating the traditional African mores and virtues. For example, he admires 'the green waters/and the ferrymen hurrying home'; he prays to 'eat with elders'; and he recalls 'the end of our journey/promising that our palms shall prosper'. Beyond these, all that haunts him is the inhibition which society places on his path. He laments:

35

Will they let me go
and pick the curing herbs behind fallen huts
to make our cure, their cure?
is the guile of the forest animal
the lingering desire of every marksman
returning from futile hunt
beaten by desert rain and thistles
on his shoulder the limpid hare
and empty guns?
to hoe our fields, plant my own corn
to wait for rain to come?
The sacrifice of years awaiting
unlit fires . . .[3]

In 'Songs of Sorrow', the poet invokes the spirit and memory of several individuals important in the tradition and culture of the people. They include Dzogbese Lisa, the supreme creator among the Ewe-speaking people; Kpeti, founder and animator of the traditional society; and Nyidevu and Kove, the dead ancestors. He appeals to them all to save the culture from total extinction. This is a poem which, while lamenting the decaying cultural values owing to foreign incursions, nostalgically and majestically celebrates those virtues which society holds dearly:

And Kpeti's great household is no more,
only the broken fence stands;
And those who dared not look in his face
Have come out as men
How well their pride is with them
Let those gone before take note
They have treated their offspring badly.[4]

Awoonor continually employs ancestral imagery to develop his theme, as in 'A Dirge':

Tell them, tell it to them
That we the children of Asiagbor's house
Went to hunt; when we returned
Our guns were pointing to the earth,
We cannot say it; someone say it for us.
Our tears cannot fall.
We have no mouths to say it with.
We took the canoe, the canoe with the sandload
They say the hippo cannot overturn.
Our fathers, the hippo has overturned our canoe
We come home
Our guns pointing to the earth.
Our mother, our dear mother
Where are our tears, where are our tears?
Give us mouth to say it, our mother.
We are on our knees to you
We are still on our knees.[5]

Asiagbor was the 'founder' of Awoonor's ancestry, while Nyidevu was his 'grandfather'. The poem also painfully articulates the poet's disappointment over the destruction and desolation of the traditional African household. The attackers of the indigenous legacy simply catch the local people unawares, leaving them totally unable to express their sorrow. This poem, much like 'Songs of Sorrow', invokes the spirit of the dead, who, apparently, would not listen to them because of certain unexplained acts of indiscretion. The piece recalls Birago Diop's 'Vanity', where the dead ancestors turn their deaf ears to the entreaties of their recalcitrant offspring.

Apart from the link between the dead and the living which the poem espouses, certain images it employs make it distinctly traditional. They include the 'hunt', the 'guns', the 'hippo', the 'sandload', 'our fathers', 'our mother' and 'We are on our knees to you'. These images successfully depict the setting of the typical African village life, and of a people who pay a great deal of respect to their forebears and cultural values.

In 'My Uncle the Diviner-Chieftain' the poet pays tribute to those elemental forces that were once the kernel on which the traditional African society was based: the 'godlike ram of sacrifices', 'the sons/you dreamt up filling your earth-space', 'father's name', 'A divination proceeds/from the diviner's good stomach', and 'older memories and fire burning'.[6]

All of the above were highly cherished and valued in traditional African society – the need to offer sacrifices to the dead ancestors, have numerous children (preferably males), adopt one's father's traditional name, and be guided in one's daily life by the divinations of soothsayers. Apparently, these cultural norms are vanishing, and in a nostalgic tone reminiscent of Kwesi Brew's, the poet – 'the messenger of that fire/the coming of the prophecy' – recalls the glamour and grace of the past.

The theme of religion also features in Awoonor's poetry. Within this broad thematic consideration is intertwined the interrelationship between soul and body and the perennial conflict between Christianity and the indigenous religion.

Much like Okigbo, Awoonor repudiates Christianity while praising the indigenous religion. But, unlike Okigbo, Awoonor not only renounces his Christian name (i.e. George Williams) as I have said earlier, but denounces Christianity with all vehemence and venom.

In 'The Cathedral' for example, Awoonor employs invectives by characterising Christianity as a 'huge senseless cathedral of doom'. On the contrary, the indigenous religion which he upholds is pure and innocent (suggested by the 'tree . . . shedding incense of the infant corn')[7]. The poet's invective against Christianity is no less dramatised in the poem 'The Weaver Bird':

>The weaver bird built in our house
>And laid its eggs on our only tree
>We did not want to send it away

We watched the building of the nest
And supervised the egg-laying.
And the weaver returned in the guise of the owner
Preaching salvation to us that owned the house
They say it came from the west
Where the storms at sea had felled the gulls
And the fishers dried their nets by lantern light
Its sermon is the divination of ourselves
And our new horizons limit at its nest
But we cannot join the prayers and answers of the
communicants
We look for new homes every day,
For new altars we strive to rebuild
The old shrines defiled by the weaver's excrement.[8]

The words 'salvation', 'sermon' and 'divination' are all echoes of Christianity, while the image the 'old shrines defiled by the weaver's excrement' connotes the indigenous religion. But what is perhaps most striking is the ingratitude displayed by the weaver bird. Rather than show appreciation for the kindness extended by the local citizenry, he desecrates their shrines and claims ownership of the household.

However, while in 'The Weaver Bird' the local people succeed in resisting the influence of Christianity (suggested by 'we cannot join the prayers of the communicants'), in the poem 'Easter Dawn' they unfortunately fall victims to the pressures of the Christian evangelists:

the gods are crying, my father's gods are crying
for a burial – for a final ritual –
but they that should build the fallen shrines
have joined the dawn marchers
singing their way towards Gethsemane
where the tear drops of agony still freshen the cactus.[9]

'Easter Dawn' resembles 'The Weaver Bird'. When the poet asserts in the latter poem, 'He has risen! Christ has risen', he leads us into several layers of meaning. Firstly, our imagination radiates between the interrelationship between body and soul, between the physical and spiritual. Secondly, we think that the soul, being of a higher philosophical order, is constantly on the move while the body is perpetually subjected to the forces of space and time.

When we link the above with what Awoonor asserts in 'The Weaver Bird' when he speaks of the 'divination of ourselves', his underlying religious motif becomes palpable: through faith and good works, man can attain a certain purity of mind and body which will enable him, like Christ, to offer salvation to his fellow men. By implication, the traditional religion, he suggests, has the same potency and force as Christianity. There is therefore no logical basis for the African to abandon his religion for a foreign faith which, as always for Awoonor, is replete with hypocrisy.

Yet in the face of such poems as 'Songs of Sorrow' and 'The Sea Eats the Land at Home', one comes to the conclusion that, although Awoonor has so much faith in the indigenous religion, he still believes strongly that it has not done enough to protect the local people and their deity from colonial assault. In the latter poem, for instance, he remonstrates:

> It is a sad thing to hear the wails,
> And the mourning shouts of the women,
> Calling on all the gods they worship,
> To protect them from the angry sea
> Aku stood outside where her cooking-pot stood,
> With her two children shivering from the cold,
> Her hands on her breast,
> Weeping mournfully
> Her ancestors have neglected her,
> Her gods have deserted her,
> It was a cold Sunday morning
> The storm was raging
> Goats and fowls were struggling in the water
> The angry water of the cruel sea.[10]

It is this note of despondency, arising from the colonial humiliation of Africa and its cultural values, that permeates much of Awoonor's religious poetry.

A third major theme of Awoonor's, and one which is closely related to the preceding theme, is the evil effect of Western colonialism generally. Much in the spirit reminiscent of David Diop's, Awoonor has a complete disdain not only for colonialism but Western civilisation as well; thus he musters all the courage at his command to satirise the white man's penetration into Africa.

Of course the effect of Western colonialism on Africa – a factor which led many African authors into writing – has serious political, social and economic dimensions. In some cases it was one of socio-economic dislocation and exploitation, usually of cash crops and mineral resources. In its worst form it reared its ugly head in such a way that the foreign writers and researchers on Africa often painted a distorted and lurid history of the continent. Indeed the evil effect of Western colonialism has every negative ramification. As Professor Killam observes:

> The primary reason for European activity in Africa was for commercial gain. The first great fortunes were made out of the slave trade and when this was abolished European powers sought legitimate trade. The search for trade brought about the scramble for Africa. White men poured into Africa. African resistance increased and armies subdued it, thus paving the way for the period of colonial rule when civil administrators conducted government ... when desultory and individual commercial enterprise gave way to chartered companies; when missionaries, confined till now for the most part to the coastal areas, were able to penetrate the interior regions of the continent in large numbers. Against this background of commercial and allied enterprise the fiction expounds a variety of personal motives.[11]

Steve Chimombo also notes:

> Europe's scramble for Africa in the last half of the nineteenth century was not only a political or economic event but it had its counterpart on the cultural plane also. African artifacts and ways of life were studied, collected, and carried like gems to be stored in European warehouses, museums, and private households. Anthropologists, linguists, missionaries, explorers, travellers, administrators descended on Africa like a horde of locusts eroding, stripping, and carrying off its cultural values.[12]

In the first place one can understand, judging from the above passages, the cause of the bitterness that marks the tone of many African writers. In the second place, all the injustices wrought on Africa above, are treated in one way or another in the works of African poets who deal with the theme of Western colonialism. We shall deal with only two aspects of these as they manifest themselves in Awoonor's poetry. The first has to do with the inherent follies of Western colonialism which Awoonor satirises. Let us examine these follies by taking a look at the poem 'We Have Found a New Land':

> The smart professionals in three piece suits
> Sweating away their humanity in dribblets
> And wiping the blood from their brow
>   We have found a new land
>   This side of eternity
>   Where our blackness does not matter
>   And our songs are dying on our lips
> Standing at hell-gate you watch those who seek admission
> Still the familiar faces that watched and gave you up
> As the one who had let the side down,
> 'Come on, old boy, you cannot dress like that'
> And tears well in my eyes for them
> Those who want to be seen in the best company
> Have abjured the magic of being themselves
> And in the new land we have found
> The water is drying from the towel
> Our songs are dead and we sell them dead to the other side
> Reaching for the Stars we stop at the house of the Moon
> And pause to relearn the wisdom of our fathers.[13]

In an interview with Robert Serumaga, Awoonor says that this poem was composed mainly to highlight the conflict of cultures between Western civilisation and the indigenous culture which the African elite has to contend with.[14] But beyond this general problem which the poem addresses, the careful reader of the piece will readily discover three aspects of Western colonialism which it satirises.

Firstly, it indicts the African elites who detest the indigenous culture while foolishly imbibing the Western lifestyle which they hardly understand. These elites are a lost generation, a pitiable species of humans who can neither fit into the European way of life nor fully identify with their own kith and kin. Secondly, the poem lampoons the racial discrimination and bigotry which are the main props of colonialism. The passage 'Where our blackness does not matter' is an ironic attack on the white man who, while studiously preaching the philosophy of the equality of all races, strongly believes in white supremacy and invincibility and the principle that 'blackness' is symptomatic of evil. Thirdly, the poet's satire is directed at the confusion which colonialism has wrought on traditional African society. Because colonialism has produced three categories of people – those loyal to the indigenous culture, those who copy the Western lifestyle, and those who are caught up between the two cultures – the African society can hardly be said to know peace: 'Our songs are dead and we sell them dead/to the other side'.

Another aspect of Western colonialism which we shall now address, and which should be of interest to most readers – partly because it is contemporary in African literary history – centres on the anti-colonial struggles put up by Africans. Basically these struggles were of two types: the one which followed the advent of the colonial incursions, and the one which occurred during the clamour for political independence. Awoonor deals with the former in 'Song of War', which he says was composed at a time when 'the Ewe fought a series of battles in a war against British occupation in the nineteenth century'.[15] And he treats the latter in the poem, 'I hold the Dreams':

```
feasts tortured smiles
after; the painful purgation
      and we sleep
      dreaming of purple paradises
      of laughter of naked virgins
in the arms of buffoons
fetid vomit
loud raucous music
rending the dream of skies
the smell of sacrifice
as the lord takes in
      the exhalations
and gathers unto himself
twelve baskets of feasted bread
      the lonely army
      lost in the city streets
Singing its last songs to sunfall

The joy, brothers, the joy!
      of waking up
      breathing the benediction
of yet another dawn.[16]
```

The struggle for political independence was one of the most painfiul and bitter aspects of Western colonialism. It was painful and bitter not only

because the colonialists, for exploitative reasons, were intransigent in giving up the colonised lands, but because for most of the time they reneged
on their promises. The way the political battle for independence was
fought, whether in Ghana, Kenya, Algeria, Uganda or elsewhere on the
African continent took different forms and demanded the best strategy
and tactics from both the colonialists and the African nationalists. If
anything, the political battle was one of 'tortured smiles' and 'painful
purgation'. Besides, it left our 'lonely army/lost in the city streets'. The
metaphor 'purple paradise' alludes to the promises of political independence made to the Africans by the colonialists but which were soon broken
with impunity at the slightest opportunity. The images, 'fetid vomit' and
'smell of sacrifice', point to the heroes and heroines among the African
nationalists who lost their lives in the political struggles. Yet, underneath
all this, is the note of optimism for the future when we shall be 'waking
up/breathing the benediction/of yet another dawn'.

Awoonor also treats the theme of love. Although as R.N. Egudu rightly
points out, this is a theme that has not caught the attention of many
critics,[17] this does not mean that the poet ignores it or that he relegates
it to the background. The apparent lack of critical attention paid to this
theme is, I think, largely due to the fact that most critics of Awoonor's
poetics have not deemed it fit to distinguish the categories of love in his
work.

Basically there are two forms of love motifs in Awoonor's verse. The
first centres on the binding relationship between man and woman. The
second focuses on the poet's intense love of his cultural roots, the kind
which J.P. Clark characterises as 'the theme of Mother Africa . . . the
theme of loss and rediscovery'.[18]

An example of Awoonor's poetry that deals with the love between man
and woman is 'Lover's Song':

> Call her, call her for me, that girl
> That girl with the neck like a desert tree
> Call her that she and I will lie in one bed.
> When you went away
> Isn't it seven years?
> Shall I fold mine and say I am cheap
> Returned unsold from the market
> If they marry a woman don't they sleep with her?
> Isn't it seven years now since you went away?[19]

The beloved wife of this poem is evidently an estranged woman who, owing
to certain inexplicable currents, has abandoned the matrimonial home.
The cause of the seven-year abandonment of the conjugal union might
have been some quarrel, ill-health, financial straits, or to the imprison-
ment of the husband. The cause might simply have been a desire to escape
the trap of marriage, but no reason is proffered. The happy news however
is that, now, the couple are united in love.

The rhetorical lines, 'Call her, call her for me, that girl/That girl with the neck like a desert tree', suggest the woman's physical attributes; presumably she is slim, tall, young and beautiful. They also project the husband's predicament: he needs the woman's love but apparently – perhaps because of the prolonged separation – he seems to have been frustrated at every turn. Characteristically, because prolonged abstinence from sexual love by couples generally intensifies emotional feelings, the poem's sentiment sounds convincing.

Other expressions in the poem develop the theme of marital love. The lines, 'Shall I fold mine and say I am cheap/Returned unsold from the market', adumbrate a note of irony. On the one hand they seem to question the sanity of prolonged marital fidelity; on the other hand, they suggest that for ethical and procreative reasons, a husband and wife must submit themselves to sexual love. The question, 'If they marry a woman don't they sleep with her?' underscores the fact that sexual love is a cardinal principle of unity in marital life. Furthermore, it highlights the pain and suffering that generally characterise the life of a separated couple. No doubt, the poem's terrain is the world of reality. It is just one example of the human love which Awoonor treats in his work.

If we turn now to Awoonor's love of his fatherland, that is, the theme of 'Mother Africa', we shall soon discover the degree to which this subject is of profound interest to him. True, he has never disguised or concealed his love of the continent. In the preface to his monumental *The Breast of the Earth: A Survey of the History, Culture and Literature of Africa South of the Sahara* (p. xiv), the poet says that the work represents his 'personal testament of and salutation to that spirit of Africa that continues through strife, tribulations, and dramatic upheavals to seek her own true self'. Earlier in this preface he explains: 'We have had to rediscover ourselves as a people. Cultural self-discovery has become an essential aspect of our new quest for self and race. Pride is part of our dream of self-awareness' (p. xiii). Nothing better articulates Awoonor's love of his fatherland than these passages.

It is against the above background that we can fully appraise Awoonor's verse that celebrates 'Mother Africa'. Indeed, several of his poems do this. For example, in 'Messages' he recollects being:

> reborn everyday in the anguish
> of a forgotten ecstasy
> long known of long shores
> stretching through childhood memories.[20]

In 'Night of My Blood', he writes:

> As we bore the million crosses
> across the vastness of time

Then they appeared, the owners of the land
Among them were the silent lovers
of nights' long harmattans;[21]

And in 'I Heard a Bird Cry', he exclaims:

I put down my white man's clothes
and rolled a cloth
To carry the ram's head
And go into the thunder house.[22]

'Messages' captures the poet's mood consumed with Africa's past which
he struggles relentlessly to re-live; 'Night of my Blood' projects the cru-
sading spirit of the dead ancestors who enjoin the living to follow their
footsteps; while in 'I Heard a Bird Cry' we are told about the way 'the protagonist rejects the European world in order to return to the right of his
fathers to achieve knowledge and understanding'.[23]

If the above three poems collectively evoke the spirit of love and affirmation for Africa's cultural values, it is in 'Rediscovery', perhaps more
than any other single poem, that the poet displays his abiding interest and
love for the traditional homeland which, to him, has a flaming sense of
destiny:

When our tears are dry on the shore
and the fishermen carry their nets home
and the seagulls return to bird island
and the laughter of the children recedes at night,
there shall still linger the communion we forged,
the feast of oneness whose ritual we partook of
There shall still be the eternal gateman
who will close the cemetery doors
and send the late mourners away.
It cannot be the music we heard that night
that still lingers in the chambers of memory
It is the new chorus of our forgotten comrades
and the hallelujahs of our second selves.[24]

Yes, 'there shall still linger the communion we forged/the feast of oneness
whose ritual we partook of'. These ringing lines embody the vortex into
which the poem's theme of love is built. In them the past and present are
interlocked. Besides, the poet presents himself as a careful recorder of
events, of the past, and of the here and now.

Other images in the poem are illuminating: they include 'chorus' and
'hallelujahs', which suggest unity, togetherness and love. Nor can the
careful reader of the poem fail to note the poet's effective employment of
antithesis, whereby the pessimistic note of the beginning is complemented

by the positive tone of the concluding lines. This device, which is very much reminiscent of Kwesi Brew's style, lifts the poem from a state of despondency and banality to one of charm and sublimity.

The theme of death and lament also features in Awoonor's poetry. Anyone fairly acquainted with his title poems – for example, 'Songs of Sorrow', 'Song of War', 'Easter Dawn', 'At the Gates' and 'A Dirge' – would observe the degree to which this theme permeates his work. Because he is pained by the nature of death generally, his verse which treats this theme is infused with lament and sorrow.

Three major kinds of death dominate Awoonor's poetry, namely: the one associated with the lack of any authentic literary 'medium'; the one which centres on the decay of Africa's cultural values; and the one which deals with the loss of human beings; particularly acquaintances or loved ones. Let us begin by looking at the first of these.

Awoonor's concern for the death of an authentic African literary 'medium', that is, from the African writer's point of view, is expressed in his poetry, essays, and polemics. For example, he shows this concern when in the preface to *The Breast of the Earth* (p. xiv), he says: 'Africa's problem today is still the problem of poverty, disease, and illiteracy'. The crucial word in this sentence is 'illiteracy'; because with an effective mass literacy programme the bulk of Africa's predicament, including 'poverty' and 'disease' can be effectively tackled. Awoonor also shows his concern for this theme in the following extract from an interview with Robert Serumaga:[25]

Serumaga: How much are you yourself, first as a person in your society, and secondly as a writer, influenced by the old traditions of the society in which you live?

Awoonor: Tremendously. I have always felt, perhaps involuntarily, I should take my poetic sensibility if you like the word from the tradition that sort of feeds my language, because in my language there is a lot of poetry, there is a lot of music and there is a lot of literary art . . . I have been brought up in English Literature, and this is a stumbling block to the exercise of forging a new language, because one is thinking about one's own language at the same time as one is thinking about English.

A poem in which Awoonor treats the theme of the death of an authentic African literary 'medium' is 'We Have Found a New Land', where he lambasts 'The smart professionals in three piece suits' who, because of their inability to forge their own style, are 'Sweating away their humanity in dribblets/And wiping the blood from their brow'.[26] He also explores this theme in 'Songs of Sorrow', where he projects a scenario of the bulk of human beings who either cannot forge their own medium of communication or have refused to do so:

The firewood of this world
Is for only those who can take heart

That is why not all can gather it.[27]

The death of Africa's cultural values, which Awoonor addresses, is very similar to that of the death of authentic artistic ambience, but they are not the same. Their similarity is no more than one of thematic coincidence. For Awoonor, the majority of Africans, particularly the elite, are dead – dead, not in the physical sense – but in the cultural sense. At best their cultural orientation is concocted or derivative. Much as they are unable to fashion their own artistic creation, so also have they lost their own soul because their cultural ambience is puerile; their cultural roots amount only to nothingness. It is this sense of cultural decay, sponsored by the African elites who would not participate in the plan to rebuild the wrecked indigenous institutions, that Awoonor satirises in 'Easter Dawn' ('they that should build the fallen shrines/have joined the dawn marchers').[28]

Let us now come to Awoonor's treatment of the beloved dead. In doing this it is important, if we are to appreciate his aesthetic range, to know something about what to him death symbolises, especially from the Ewe background which is the source of much of his poetic influence. He explains: 'Death in the Ewe imagination, is seen as a warrior, a predator who refuses money and all other things and insists upon man ... he declares war upon a household and does not stop until he reduces the homestead to ruins.'[29] This conception of death recalls the medieval *ubi sunt* motif which views mutability as a universal leveller of all creatures.

Here and there in his verse Awoonor eulogises the beloved dead. In 'Songs of Sorrow', he laments the passing away of Agosu, 'the tree on which I lean'.[30] And in 'A Dirge' he celebrates the death of Ashiagbor, 'founder of my lineage' who died because 'the hippo has overturned our canoe'.[31] The ominous reference to the hippo capsizing the canoe indicts the dead ancestors who, according to the Ewe culture,[32] are expected to offer protection to the living against imminent disaster but failed to do so.

Awoonor also treats the problem of death in 'At the Gates':

Don't cry for me
my daughter, death called her
it is an offering of my heart
the ram has not come to stay
three days and it has gone
elders and chiefs whom will I trust
a snake has bitten my daughter
whom will I trust?
walk on gently; give me an offering
that I will give it to God
and he will be happy.

Uproot the yams you planted
for everything comes from God

it is an evil god who sent me
that all I have done
I bear the magic of the singer that has come
I have no paddle, my wish,
to push my boat into the river.[33]

The above lines lament the death of the poet's daughter, who has apparently been killed by a snake bite. To the poet, God gives and takes; therefore he cannot question His will. This is the wise man's philosophical way of viewing the baffling phenomenon of death. It is a devastating, yet consoling, experience. The phrase, 'an offering of my heart/the ram', is a definite Biblical allusion to Abraham's willingness to offer Isaac for divine sacrifice. Also, 'I bear the magic of the singer that has come/I have no paddle, my wish,/to push my boat into the river', suggests the poet's limitations in the midst of death. These allusions, apart from their coordinates of pain, endurance and self-mockery, inform the poem's structure with a poignancy reminiscent of the classical tradition where the elegist identifies his own role in the face of tragedy and sorrow.

Awoonor's accomplishment as a poet is that as a major African writer who believes strongly in the culture of his people and who articulates his themes from the perspectives of cultural ambience, his verse is bound to appeal increasingly to his future readers rather than to past or contemporary ones, for its intensity, originality and persuasiveness.

NOTES

1. Kofi Awoonor, *The Breast of the Earth: A Survey of the History, Culture and Literature of Africa South of the Sahara* (New York and London: Nok Publishers, 1975): 202.
2. Ken Goodwin, *Understanding African Poetry* (London: Heinemann, 1982): 93.
3. K.E. Senanu and T. Vincent, eds, *A Selection of African Poetry* (Harlow, U.K.: Longman, 1976): 150.
4. Awoonor, *The Breast of the Earth*: 203–4.
5. Awoonor, *The Breast of the Earth*: 209.
6. K.E. Senanu and T. Vincent, *A Selection of African Poetry*: 153.
7. K.E. Senanu and T. Vincent, *A Selection of African Poetry*: 144.
8. Gerald Moore and Ulli Beier, eds., *Modern Poetry from Africa* (Harmondsworth: Penguin, 1976): 102.
9. Moore and Beier: 103.
10. Moore and Beier: 101.
11. G.D. Killam, *Africa in English Fiction 1874–1939* (Ibadan: Ibadan University Press, 1968): 4–5.
12. Steve Chimombo, 'Oral Literature Research in Malawi, 1870–1986', *Research in African Literatures*, 18, **4** (Winter 1987): 487–8.
13. Senanu and Vincent: 147–8.

14. Dennis Duerden and Cosmo Pieterse, eds., *African Writers Talking* (London: Heinemann, 1978): 30.
15. Awoonor, *The Breast of the Earth*: 214–5.
16. Kofi Awoonor and G. Adali-Mortty, eds., *Messages: Poems from Ghana*, (London: Heinemann, 1979): 77.
17. R.N. Egudu, *Four Modern West African Poets* (New York and London: Nok Publishers, 1977): 70.
18. J.P. Clark, *The Example of Shakespeare* (Evanston: Northwestern University Press, 1970): 45.
19. Moore and Beier: 102.
20. Awoonor, *Messages*: 18.
21. Awoonor: 86.
22. Awoonor, *The Breast of the Earth*: 211.
23. Awoonor: 211.
24. Awoonor and Adali-Mortty: 76.
25. Duerden and Pieterse: 30–1.
26. Senanu and Vincent: 147.
27. Awoonor, *The Breast of the Earth*: 203. Awoonor's explanatory notes (p. 206) to these quoted lines say in part: 'Those who can gather any must be strong of heart and firm of spirit . . . The use of this image to focus an abstract philosophical thought again illustrates the reliance upon the commonplace experience or the blatantly obvious for poetic statement.'
28. Moore and Beier: 103.
29. Awoonor, *The Breast of the Earth*: 207.
30. Awoonor: 204.
31. Awoonor: 209.
32. Awoonor: 209.
33. Awoonor, *Messages*: 80.

Niyi Osundare's Poetry & the Yoruba Oral Artistic Tradition

Aderemi Bamikunle

The oral traditions, often called oral literature and more recently orature, refer specifically in this essay, to 'traditional songs, song–poems, various forms of oral narratives, tales, legends, myths, historical narratives, [and] the creative arts generally in which part of the concern is the rendering of events in a manner that gives aesthetic pleasure'[1]. The emphasis in this essay will be the aesthetic elements of these oral traditional artistic forms as it tries to see in what ways the poetry of Niyi Osundare, a major voice in new Nigerian poetry, has used materials and techniques from the oral traditions. The assumption here is that 'the modern African writer can be influenced by the principles [of artistic production] or style of [oral] art, and other forms of oral traditions'. This influence, as Joel Adedeji emphasised in 'Folklorism in Contemporary Nigerian Dramatic Arts',[2] is almost unavoidable for the modern African writer. The attraction to the oral traditions is 'the product of a movement the main motive of which proceeds from the consciousness of contemporary artists to work out of the traditions and heritage of our own people bearing in mind the need to be relevant in forging the link between the people's [unwritten] ethos and the new horizons of the times'.[3]

There are many areas in which the modern writer may be influenced by the artistic practices of oral traditions. A writer searching for an alternative social vision to the degenerate and degenerating contemporary socio-political system may accept the classless egalitarian worldview or social vision of village communities as expressed in their works. This is what Osundare does in *Village Voices*[4] and to some extent in *The Eye of the Earth*.[5] Sometimes the traditional worldview may be criticised or satirised in order to point out lessons to be learnt from its shortcomings, as Soyinka does in *The Strong Breed*[6] and the *Swamp Dwellers*;[7] as Osofisan does in *No more the Wasted Breed* in *Morountodun and Other Plays*[8], and Sowande does in 'A Sanctus for Women' in *Farewell to Babylon and Other Plays*.[9] These playwrights see traditional religious myths as smokescreens behind which authorities operate very perverse social ideologies of oppression and exploitation. By exposing these myths

49

they undermine the social vision that they embody. These are the major ways in which traditional social vision can influence the modern writer.

But by far the most common use made of oral traditions is in the area of artistic forms. Most African writers, as Oyin Ogunba has said in 'Traditional African Festival Drama',[10] value traditional arts more for their artistic values than for their social and religious views. They often adapt the story line of myths and traditional dramatic idiom to interpret contemporary life as in Soyinka's 'Idanre'[11] and *A Dance of the Forests*[12] or Jack Mapanje's *Of Chameleons and Gods.*[13] African writers also find traditional 'works' a rich source of imagery – simile, metaphor, symbolism, proverbs, personification and other forms of language. Many an African writer has found himself exploring various forms of traditional language use. Finally, artists, especially poets, find the prosodic system of oral poetry in African languages very useful in their experimentation with poetic form.

In coming to Osundare's relationship to the oral traditions one must be reminded that the oral traditions do not belong only in the past as many critics presume. Even in the works of the renowned critic of oral literature Isidore Okpewho, oral literature seems to be thought of as belonging to the past. This is still very much the case in his recent article 'African Poetry: The Modern Writer and the Oral Tradition'.[14] Such references in that article to 'the old forms', 'writers reinstating their heritage', oral traditions 'leaning heavily on contemporary field evidence' as writers 'gear toward recovering the traditional image of the poet', and the writer's speculation that 'there is good reason to believe that this [the oral tradition] was pretty much the way things were before the coming of the Arabs and the Europeans' suggests that oral traditions belong to the past. On the other hand Osundare's poetic practices suggest that there is a contemporary phase of oral traditions existing side by side with the modern written literatures of Africa. They can still be seen and heard everywhere in Africa as vibrant forms of art. Osundare borrows from these contemporary arts in his poems, as we will see in the analysis of *Village Voices* and *The Eye of the Earth.*

The influence of the oral traditions on contemporary Nigerian poetry is apparent in the works of the major writers, Tanure Ojaide (*Children of Iroko*,[15] *Labyrinths of the Delta*,[16] *Eagle's Vision*[17]), Osofisan (*Minted Coins*[18]) and Osundare, (particularly in *Village Voices, The Eye of the Earth*). But it is not true, as Ojaide says in his article 'The Changing Voice of History: Contemporary African Poetry',[19] that it is the new generation of Nigerian and African writers who started a concerted coherent and consistent use of the oral traditions in modern writing. One cannot miss the importance of Yoruba oral traditions in Soyinka's poetry, or the recourse to Igbo mythology and culture in Okigbo's *Labyrinths.* As for Clark, he gives an indication of his indebtedness to traditions in *A Reed in the Tide*[20] by the proverbs which he has made famous. 'Two hands does a man have.' His poetry shows a good fusion of traditional and Western elements of poetry. It is true that the products of the fusion of the African oral traditions and Western forms of poetry in the works of the older African poets are never really like or sound like their African traditional predecessors. Instead the poems sound and look more like Western modernist poems. It is for this reason that Chinweizu et al in *Toward the Decolonisation of African Literature*[21] have accused the older generation of Euro-centricism in their works. By contrast, the new generation of Nigerian and African poets have moved relatively closer to their African tradition models in their use of imagery and form and prosody. Osundare's poetry manifests this remarkable use of the oral traditions.

An indication of his desire to produce poetry that is close to traditional poetry and to reject poetry that is too intellectual, erudite and elitist, comes early in his poetic career. In 'Poetry is', the opening poem of his first published collection, he rejects the kind of poetry written by his predecessors on the Nigerian poetic scene as too inaccessible to be good poetry. His imagery shows his disenchantment with this kind of poetry. Poetry should not be

> ... the esoteric whisper
> Of an excluding tongue
> not a claptrap
> for a wondering audience
> not a learned quiz
> entombed in Graeco-Roman lore.

The poetry he will write is described in images that point towards traditional poetry with a strong consideration for a communal audience. The images, 'hawker's ditty', 'the lyric of the marketplace', 'the eloquence of the gong' remind readers of the traditional contexts of artistic performance. The images remind us that his art, as is typical of traditional art, is meant for everyone in society. 'The gong' symbol of the desired communal involvement is traditionally recognised as a medium of art serving the community. In Osundare's ideal, 'Poetry' is 'man/meaning to/man'. With this introduction, *Songs of the Marketplace*[22] is meant to be popular poetry rendered in 'popular' art form shared by the community. His poetry is best appreciated as developing towards achieving this ideal.

The central preoccupation of his poetry is thus established in this first collection: the concern he feels for the suffering and deprivations of the masses; the disgust he feels for their exploiters and oppressors, the politicians; and the hope he harbours of the oppressed overturning the system to their own advantage. The subject matter of this collection is common enough, as the poet or his poetic persona quests through his society exposing one social malaise after another: the social suffering and deprivation of the masses ('Excursions') large scale maladministration and mismanagement ('Sule Chase'), political fraud ('Rithmetic Ruse', 'Siren'). Everywhere the poet goes, the university ('Publish or Perish'), the Railway Corporation ('The Nigerian Railway'), the civil service ('Excursions') the story is the same, fraud on a pervasive large scale, inefficiency and mismanagement in high places with the masses bearing the burden of the fraudulent mismanagement of the leaders.

With regard to his poetic ideal, this first collection is accessible poetry, whose main strengths are its vivid descriptions, powerful imagery and relentless sarcasm, as in:

> We see village boys' Kwashiorkor bellies
> hairless heads impaled on pin necks
> and ribs baring the benevolence
> of the body politic (p. 7)

The difference between the rich and the poor and the general state of social neglect is captured in the lines:

> Several government people
> have passed through these streets
> several mercedes tyres have drenched
> gaunt road liners in sewer water
> several sanitary inspectors have come
> in formidable helmets and gas masks
> but rot and tanwiji* escape
> the uniformed eye. (p. 9)
>
> *(Yoruba for mosquito larvae)

The satiric irony and mocking sarcasm which give power to his poetry are evident in this description of deliberate inefficiency:

> I have been through
> the secretariat
> where civil servants
> are all but civil
> here files are
> lost and found
> found and lost
> by mysterious messengers' magic.
>
> The correspondence tray
> is the coffin of ailing democracy
> pending
> is heavier than
> Out
> and both together are leaner than
> IN. (p. 12)

But in this collection we find only very rudimentary usage of poetic forms from oral traditions, the only form consistently used is the proverb. Very often, as in this first stanza from the poem, 'Ignorance', the proverb is a translation from Yoruba lore, and in its position in the poem it provides the background of traditional wisdom or maxim against which the foolishness of contemporary social practice is viewed and condemned.

The cow is dying
for a trip to London
let it go
it will come back
as corned beef

This is an appropriate image for a man who paradoxically is the architect of his own doom. It combines with the image of an archetypal character from Yoruba myth to describe the politician who rules ever his subjects by exploiting their ignorance. Madaru is the personification of confusion, the name of the man who delights in scattering rather than gathering together:

Madaru buys a crown
and becomes a king
And you ask
how could sheep all agree
to give their crown to a wolf?

The usage of this form (often translations from Yoruba proverbs) is to be found in some stanzas of 'Udoji', the first two stanzas and the last stanza of 'Reflections', stanzas one, three and four of 'To the Dinosaur' and the last two stanzas of 'on Seeing A Benin Mask In A British Museum'. In its consistent use of the proverbial form, in its juxtaposing of the proverbial wisdom of the people with the injudicious actions of political and administrative leaders, thereby assessing these actions and exposing their foolishness, *Songs of the Marketplace* anticipates *Village Voices* where the various forms of oral tradition provide the predominant poetic technique.

In many respects it is in *Villages Voices* that Osundare realises his ideals in poetry. Here his social vision based on the socio-political values of the traditional village life (a vision which he juxtaposes with the urban-based 'dog eat dog' contemporary socio-political system) finds perfect expression in the artistic forms of oral tradition. The organising impulse for the poems is the revolutionary confrontation between rural man with his (somewhat idealised) vision of life and the oppressive, exploitative neo-colonialist national political administration. By this confrontational jux-tapositioning the poet uses tradition to assess the value of modern civilisation and governance, in order to condemn it. In order to allow the voice of tradition full scope to do this Osundare adopts a poetic posture that modernists will call the posture of impersonality. His poetic voice is sub-sumed under the communal voice as he prefers to speak through various

personae from the rural areas who adapt various forms of traditional art
to denounce the national capitalist system.

The basic qualities of the traditional vision of life are love of labour
and of social equality, contentment with little and communal concern.
The rural society lives by and delights in what it produces for itself and
boasts:

> These hands
> have subdued stubborn jungles
> unmasked fertile groves
> and plumbed the seedful promise
> of loam plains ('Cradling Hands')

Going hand in hand with this is the lack of desire to be above others, lord-
ing it over others:

> Let me be
> a grass in the meadow
> matching heads with others
> to repel oppressive storms
> with stalks steeled by shared resolve
>
> Let me be
> an active grip
> in a hand of equal fingers ('A Grass in the Meadow')

There is no desire for excessive acquisition of wealth. In poverty, they are
as content as in plenty and remain one in the solidarity of the poor. In
'Akintude, Come Home', rather than allow a member of the rural community to suffer want in the city, the community invites him to

> Come back here
> where the walls are mud
> and meatless meals quiet
> the howling stomach.

But also, there is self-confidence in the rural man's ability to take on the
central administration and win because of their knowledge of their place
in the political economy. The image of the cat, slow but deadly when
necessary describes this confidence:

> Let no-one mistake our sleep
> for a stupor of death
> the slowness of the cat
> is skill
> not a lack
> of will:

He produces that which sustains the affluence of the city:

the funds for our community centre
built your palace
the funds for our rugged roads
bought your car
the funds for our water scheme
irrigate your banks in Europe ('Unequal Fingers')

From this realisation of its strength comes the confident threat to the system:

We shall rip down the stars today
and give them a second eye
we will then hold them in
our own hands
and make them shine our will

If the stars are
We make them be ('The Stars Did It')

It is from this rural vision that Osundare satirises the lack of progress in twenty-five years of independence ('Sleeping, at Five and Twenty'); the duplicity of politicians ('The Politician's Two Mouths', 'The Chicken Story', 'Dying Another's Death'); their greed ('Eating with all the Fingers', 'Eating Tomorrow's Yam'); their trickery or political chicanery ('A Villager's Protest'); their taste for foreign goods ('The Eunuch's Child'); and the social contradictions of the administrative system beggaring the producers to enrich Government loafers ('The New Farmer's Bank' and 'A Farmer on Seeing Cocoa House, Ibadan').

Because Osundare is seeing the rest of society through the vision of the rural man, the art forms which had always represented this vision are particularly important in *Village Voices* as is indicated in the first poem, 'I wake up this Morning' where he restates his ideals of poetry. As we see in his first collection the ideals are symbolised by objects relating to traditional art: the image of 'the towncrier' with his instrument of art 'the gong' symbolises the poet's adoption of the people's art and art forms. Thus he explores the various forms of oral tradition more in this collection than he does in any other book. He does not use the poet's lyrical voice, instead he talks to us through personae who truly represent the voice of tradition. The borrowings from tradition range from the use of familiar images and symbols, to fables and the morality they preach or vision they express ('The Chicken Story'), the proverb form ('Eating Tomorrow's Yam'), the traditional form of songs of abuse – song duel – ('A Dialogue of the Drums'), praise poetry ('I Wake up this Morning') and the use of Yoruba maxims ('The Eunuch's Child').

When Osundare uses a proverb or a maxim he uses not only the prosodic form but also the content, the morality or social insight it contains to contrast or judge the prevalent social malaise around him. In 'The Politician's Two Mouths', the very title which suggests duplicity is a rendering of a Yoruba saying. So also is another central image contained in this transposition of a Yoruba proverb:

Alas: a thin membrane covers the belly
We cannot see the inside of a lying wolf

which suggests the impossibility of knowing the true intention of the politicians. It is against this central image that the trickery of the Nigerian politician is revealed. This is a characteristic use of Yoruba proverbs and wise sayings. Frequently, as in this poem, the poet uses the rhetorical devices of the delivery of proverbs, for greater effect: 'Is it not the politician/who sees a snake/and hails an earthworm?' The poetic effect of the image here, though it is the poet's rather than from tradition, is to re-affirm the image of the politician already established by the Yoruba proverbs. Often the form of the proverb used is a free rendering in English. But the rendering which retains its essential images remains recognisable to the Yoruba speaker and its form even in the translation remains obviously proverbial. This is what happens in the first stanza of the poem, 'The Eunuch's Child' a poem which talks about the foreign tastes of the politician:

The Eunuch's Child lives
in a land beyond the seas
he will mount the saddle
of the waves, someday
and bring him back
in a galloping boat

In its original form the proverb talks of the tendency of the eunuch to situate his claims in far off places where such claims cannot be verified. The poet uses the free translation to satirise the preference for foreign tastes for which the politician has squandered the profits of the oil boom. Generally, Osundare uses the proverb as a kernel or core image that the rest of the poem elaborates and expands upon.

What he does with many well known Yoruba satirical songs is similar to what he does with the proverb. Osundare's criticism of the police force, itself a victim of the political 'drama of oppression' but which allows itself to be used to brutalise the populace, is rendered against the background of a close translation of a popular song that apparently derives from prisoners' work songs:

The warder's wife never bears a proper baby
The warder's wife never does
If she doesn't give birth to a truncheon
She delivers a lunatic
The warder's wife never has a proper child.

Sometimes the whole poem is simply a translation from traditional material. Such is the poem 'The Bride's Song', a bride's farewell song to her parents and relations. The song is a celebration of the values that women cherish in traditional life: barns full of yams and stores of grain from the hands of a husband who loves labour; virile male with 'children between his groins' and 'children playing in the moonlight'. The primacy of children in traditional life is imaged in the translations of Yoruba names, 'Child is honour' (Omoniyi) and 'Child is gold' (Wuralomo). The last two lines are translations of a popular prayer for brides by well-wishers wishing the bride a life of comfort, not the hardship of having to sleep on a comfortless mat.

Two other traditions of songs have influences on Osundare's poems in *Village Voices* – praise poetry and songs of abuse. Their influences are to be found particularly in 'I Wake Up this Morning', 'A Dialogue of the Drums' and 'Not in my Season of Songs'. There are two forms of praise poetry that Osundare uses, the poetry of self praise, and the traditional eulogy of others. The poetry of self praise is found in 'A Dialogue of Drums' where the poet contends with 'palace singers', prophets of false art who serve the leaders. The techniques he uses from tradition are, on the one hand, the use of hyperbolic images to project a heroic image of himself:

> I was born with a song in my throat
> And my hands on the face of the drum
> I have thrilled royal steps
> With *gbedu*'s majestic accent
> And learnt why *egiri* turns thick ears
> To the hunter's feeble arrows
> I have put a stick to *ibembe*
> Urging virgin brides to dance to
> The virtue between their legs
> When I raise my voice
> The world joins the chorus

While, on the other hand, his enemies, the apostles of false art, undergo a process of mock-heroic deflation in derogatory images: 'their hippo hands slap the drum', 'flogging mere noise' in 'excess juvenile praise' to praise those 'whose words/behead the world'. They are 'like vultures bald as/the drums they beat', always after the rewards of 'miserable ceremonies'. Another poem which uses the traditional model of song duels and songs of abuse is 'Not in My Season of Songs' where the writer continues his assault on false art and false artists. Here, as in certain types of poems of traditional songs of abuse the poet uses an indirect form of lampooning to run down his enemies. He tells his enemy he is not in the mood for a fight, not in his 'Season of Songs' but the whole poem is an unrelenting rain of insults. His enemy has 'crooked finger', 'swollen testicles', 'lips thick like hippo skin', his mother has 'elephant legs', his 'buffalo head' father was a 'shit carrier', a slave driver for the 'Whiteman', his uncle 'looks like/a bag of cocoa with a small ball for a head'. The influence of panegyric poetry is seen in the use of the form of formulaic lines familiar in traditional panegyric poetry with its system of parallelisms and repetitions:

> He who has not seen the sea
> let him taste salt in the soup
> he who does not know fire
> let him watch a forest blaze
> in the season before the rains
> he who does not know the poet
> let him listen to the footsteps of words

In addition to the use of these forms of Yoruba oral tradition, there is also the pervasive use of traditional images drawn largely from the flora and fauna and the general environment of traditional life and cosmology: images of the chicken in the 'The Chicken Story', of the cock's flame of fire in 'The Cock's Comb of Fire', of the snake 'sloughing/the burden of bygone years' in 'New Birth' representing the possibility of a new order, the image of the cat as a symbol of will and skill in spite of its slowness in 'Listen, Book Wizards', of the stars as symbol of the ruse of the preaching of fate, destiny and pre-ordination in 'The Stars Did It', of the 'Iroko' king of the forest as symbol of political tyranny in 'A Grass in the Meadow'. Indeed there is no striking poetic image in *Village Voices* that is not drawn from the oral traditions.

Osundare continues the celebration of traditional culture in *The Eye of the Earth* but in a different mode from *Village Voices*. The most obvious difference is that in *The Eye of the Earth* he assumes his own poetic voice. He speaks as the prodigal, the alienated man, once 'jilted from the farmstead' returning to the traditional society of his youth, to a stage of the traditional culture which was before the 'Cancerous god called MONEY' from the West 'smashed old customs'. The organising impulse of *The Eye of the Earth* is the journey motif. The substance of the collection is the 'journey into these times [youth of the poet] and beyond' a journey 'into the house of memory'. The central preoccupation is to contrast what life meant in those times when 'Earth was ours and we earth's', with what life means in contemporary times when after the destruction of the 'Core of [their] ancient humanistic ethos', commercialism and 'the god of money' have forced a desecration of the earth, the bedrock of ancient customs and culture:

> Lynched
>   the lakes
> Slaughtered
>   the Seas
> Mauled
>   the mountains ('Our Earth Will Not Die')

In contrast to this the poet shows the traditional sacred respect for the earth because of the closeness to the earth and dependence on the earth for everything both in life and death:

> Temporary basement
> and lasting roof
>
> First clayey coyness
> and last alluvial joy
>
> breadbasket
> and compost.

The closeness to the earth also means a love for labour: 'we grew what we ate and ate what we grew'. The joy of labour, of being able to create oneself through one's labour is sensuously expressed in 'Farmer-Born':

> Farmer-born peasant bred
> I have frolicked from furrow to furrow
> Sounded kicking tubers in the Womb
> of quickening earth
> and fondled the melon breasts
> of succulent ridges

The images suggest something akin to a sexual relationship between traditional man and the earth, and the produce of the earth is the result of such a relationship. In contemporary times under pressure to produce for cash, the warm relationship has given way to coldness: 'With our earth so warm/How can our hearth be so cold?' The poet asks in dismay:

> Where are they
> the yam pyramids which challenged the sun
> in busy barns
> where are the
> pumpkins which caressed earthbreast
> like mammary burdens ('Harvestcall')

As the poet takes us through the seasons and diurnal rounds of social activities it is apparent that he seeks to make us see and feel the way that traditional man sees and feels about his environment – the earth, the forests and hills and rivers and animals. To do this the writer explores the visions of living as expressed in the oral traditions. Central to this vision is the polytheism implied in rural man's relationship to nature. In the preface, Osundare had talked of 'the terrifyingly green' vegetation in which everything and being 'had its name in the baffling baptism of Nature'. The rocks are more than rocks, they are a 'creative, material essence', as 'guardians of the harvest spirit', as 'lasting [as] time and space'. The rains, 'The giver and sustainer of life', the poet says 'occupy

a god-like place in the consciousness of Ikere's agrarian people'. The dominant method by which Osundare suggests the 'living' essence of nature is
by the use of personification through which he animates every element of
it, thus producing some of the most exciting nature poetry in Africa. Every
quality of every aspect of nature is realised through the analogical images
of human action. This technique is used effectively for example in this
celebration of the chameleon's ability to change its dress at will:

> Don this praying mantis
> in its eternal tabernacle
> wringing green hands before
> an absent god
> Don the unlistening forest
> salaaming (instead) to the
> compelling muezzin of a loud
> insistent wind.
> Don this praying brood
> this school of dancing twigs
> Don this brood, praying
> like a flock of green aladuras
> in their noise-and-sand retreat ('Forest Echoes')

The same technique is used to describe the destruction of nature in 'Our
Earth Will Not Die':

> a lake is killed by the arsenic urine
> from the bladder of profit factories
> a poisoned stream staggers down the hills
> coughing chaos in the sickly sea
> the wailing whale, belly up like a frying fish
> crests the chilling swansong of parting waters.

Another remarkable device from oral tradition is the prescription of
musical accompaniment to the poems: 'Forest Echoes', for example, is to
be accompanied with 'flute and heavy drums', 'The Rocks Rose to Meet
Me' to be 'chanted with "agba drum" throbbing in the background',
'Harvestcall' 'to be chanted to lively bata music'. One cannot truly assess
the effect of this on the poems until one has seen a performance but this
is an indication of Osundare's desire to move closer and closer to performance poetry in the tradition of ritual drama and ritual poetry.

Osundare uses the oral traditions far more than many other writers.
Not only has he used the many forms of art from the oral traditions as core
elements in his poetic technique in *Village Voices* and to some extent, *The
Eye of the Earth*, but he has also proved in the two books of poetry that the
oral traditions can 'provide for a meaningful critique of the contemporary
problems'. In his hands traditional social vision has become a weapon for
very incisive criticism of contemporary political economy. Also his
judicious use of elements of the African oral tradition, has produced

poetry that is distinctively African. There are definitely problems and limitations to attempts at transposing elements from the oral traditions to the written traditions in a non-African language. But the example of Osundare, and the Ghanaian poetic experiments by Atukwei Okai[23] and Kofi Anyidoho[24] have proved that African poetry can gain in strength and distinctiveness by appropriating techniques and qualities from African performance poetry and dramatic ritual.

NOTES

1. Aderemi Bamikunle, 'Folklore and the Challenges of National Integration' (Proceedings of the 5th Annual Congress of the Nigerian Folklore Society, Zaria, 1985): 327.
2. Joel Adedeji, 'Folkloricism in Contemporary Nigerian Dramatic Arts' (Proceedings of the 5th Annual Congress of the Nigerian Folklore Society, Zaria, 1985): 251–276.
3. Adedeji: 251–2.
4. Niyi Osundare, *Village Voices* (Ibadan: Evans Brothers, 1984).
5. Niyi Osundare, *The Eye of the Earth* (Ibadan: Heinemann, 1986).
6. Wole Soyinka, 'The Strong Breed', in *Three Plays* (Ibadan: Three Crown, 1963).
7. Wole Soyinka, 'The Swamp Dwellers', in *Three Plays* (Ibadan: Three Crowns, 1963).
8. Femi Osofisan, *Morountodun and Other Plays* (Ibadan: Heinemann, 1985).
9. Bode Sowande, *Farewell to Babylon and Other Plays* (Ibadan: Longman Drumbeat, 1981).
10. Oyin Ogunba, 'Traditional African Festival Drama', in *Theatre in Africa*, eds. Ogunba and Irele (Ibadan: Ibadan University Press, 1978).
11. Wole Soyinka, 'Idanre', *Idanre and Other Poems* (London: Eyre/Methuen, 1967).
12. Wole Soyinka, *A Dance of the Forests* (Oxford: Ibadan University Press, 1963).
13. Jack Mapanje, *Of Chameleons and Gods* (Ibadan: Heinemann, 1981).
14. Isidore Okpewho, 'African Poetry: The Modern Writer and the Oral Tradition', *African Literature Today*, 16 (1988).
15. Tanure Ojaide, *Children of Iroko* (New York: Greenfield Review Press, 1973).
16. Tanure Ojaide, *Labyrinths of the Delta* (New York: Greenfield Review Press, 1983).
17. Tanure Ojaide, *Eagle's Vision* (Detroit: Lotus Press, 1987).
18. Femi Osofisan, *Minted Coins* (Ibadan: Heinemann, 1987).
19. Tanure Ojaide, 'The Changing Voice of History: Contemporary African Poetry' in *Geneva–Africa*, 27, 1 (1989).
20. J.P. Clark, *A Reed in the Tide* (London: Longman, 1967).
21. Chinweizu et al, *Toward the Decolonisation of African Literature* (Enugu: Fourth Dimension, 1980).
22. Niyi Osundare, *Songs of the Marketplace* (Ibadan: New Horn Press, 1983).
23. Atukwei Okai, *Lorgorlighi Lorgarhythms* (Tema: Ghana Publishing Corporation, 1974).
24. Kofi Anyidoho, *Earth Child* (Accra: Woeli Publishing Services, 1985).

Plot & Conflict
in African Folktales

Sam Ukala

The appreciation of the African folktale has, since the late nineteenth century, been predominantly from the theoretical perspectives of Evolutionism, Diffusionism, Structural-Functionalism and Psychoanalysis.[1] Although these have been largely discredited because of their highly speculative nature and inadequate concern with aesthetic value, some of their features, specifically, their classification systems or typology (related to Diffusionism) and their functionality, including that of providing psychological escape (related to Structural-Functionalism and Psychoanalysis), still linger on in African contemporary folktale scholarship.[2] More attention has, however, been focused on the modes of transmitting the folktale.

But there is more to literary appreciation than classification (based on motif or form), determination of function, and description of modes of transmission. The quality of a literary story or a play does not, in fact, emanate from its thematic class or function or mode of transmission, but from its crafting, the skill that has gone into the moulding and joining of its component parts. Hence a critical examination of plot, conflict, language, characterisation and thought has been paramount in the assessment of the literary short story, the novel and the play. But this critical method is, surprisingly, hardly encountered in African folktale scholarship. With regard to the language of the folktale, for example, interest has hardly been shown beyond the ideophone. Issues of authenticity and reliability[3] may militate against a structural, lexical and semantic analysis of the folktale in translation, but a similar analysis of the original language may hold greater rewards than may at first appear likely. And the plot, conflict, characterisation and thought in a translated folktale may be studied with even less risk of being hampered by considerations of authenticity and reliability. The neglect of the task of analysing the folktale as literary art makes it appear as if hardly anything remains to be said of the folktale after Sigmund Freud. This paper is, primarily, a call to reverse this trend; it points to new challenges to students of the folktale. However, it concentrates only on the two aspects of plot and conflict, partly because of the constraints of space and partly because they constitute the usual point of take-off in studies of this nature.

Plot

Aristotle defines plot as 'the arrangement of the incidents' in a literary work of art and recognises two kinds of plot, simple and complex.[4] He describes the simple plot as one in which the action is 'continuous' and 'without peripeteia' or 'recognition'. He defines peripeteia, as 'a change by which the action veers round to its opposite, subject always to the rule of probability or necessity' and recognition as 'a change from ignorance to knowledge'.[5] A complex plot, according to Aristotle, is, therefore, one in which a change in the action is accompanied by peripeteia or recognition or both.[6] In other words, the simple plot is advanced in one direction and its events are arranged in such a way that one could predict how they would end, while the complex plot is initially advanced the same way as the simple plot until one or two twists are introduced at a crucial moment, which thwart predictions that may have been made of future events. A third kind of plot, the compound plot, has been recognised since Aristotle. It has two or more progressions of events which are finally compounded into an aesthetic whole. The simple, complex and compound plots are exemplified by Marlowe's *Doctor Faustus*, Sophocles' *King Oedipus* and Shakespeare's *The Tempest*, respectively.[7]

In African folktales, there seem to be three kinds of plot also. What corresponds to the simple plot, we shall call the single plot. Then there are the double plot and the multiple plot, neither of which corresponds to the complex or the compound plot. Most African folktales are of the single plot kind. For example, out of the sixty Ika[8] folktales collected by this writer as part of the data for this work, forty-six, that is approximately seventy-seven per cent, are of this type. Other samples of the single-plot folktale are 'Fourteen Hundred Cowries', 'The Boy and the Piece of Yam', 'The Hen and the Hawk', 'The Elephant and the Cock', 'The Wrestling Contest Between the Cat and the Tortoise' in Abayomi's *Fourteen Hundred Cowries*,[9] and the nine tales in Chapter 7 and the eleven in Chapter 8 of Knappert's *Myths and Legends*.[10] In fact, most of the tales in the two collections have single plots. In each single-plot tale, there is a unidirectional progression of sequential events from a natural beginning to a predictable end – 'natural beginning' here, is the point at which there has been a motivation for the protagonist to embark on an enterprise which elicits the central action of the tale.

Let us examine closely one of our examples of a single-plot folktale, 'The Wrestling Contest Between the Cat and the Tortoise' in Abayomi's *Fourteen Hundred Cowries*. Motivated by envy, Tortoise persistently courts the friendship of Cat, the popular wrestling champion of the animal kingdom. When he eventually obtains this, he entertains Cat lavishly and apparently worms his way into Cat's confidence. Then he asks Cat to tell him the secret of his wrestling power and Cat tells him that he has two jujus (whereas, in fact, he has three). Tortoise soon begins to use the two jujus and to defeat all comers in contest after contest. Emboldened by conceit, he challenges Cat. Each of their first two bouts ends in a draw because the contestants employ the same juju simultaneously. In the third and final bout, Tortoise uses a combination of the first and second jujus while Cat uses the third juju. Cat wins. The tortoise's enterprise begins with a motivation, which is, in his circumstances, natural. It is easy to predict how he would exploit the Cat's friendship, therefore, even if the cat does not reveal his third juju. And as soon as that revelation is withheld, one predicts, rightly, the outcome of the tortoise's enterprise.

The double plot is of two sub-kinds. The first is a unilinear link-up of two single plots. The link may be provided by motivation – which means that the two plots may be identically motivated – or by setting, by a major character, or a combination of these. The second sub-kind of the double plot is rare. It is a juxtaposition of two contrasting single plots, at the beginning of which is a common motivation.

'Tortoise in Cow's Belly', an Ika folktale, is an example of a double-plot tale which is a unilinear link-up of two single plots. Motivated by greed, Tortoise eats up Cow's maize seeds while pretending to be helping to plant them. When Cow eventually discovers this, he makes up his mind to go secretly to Tortoise's farm to eat up his luxuriant maize. But Tortoise had read Cow's plan from his face and had rushed to the farm to hide in an ear of maize. Cow grazes on until he swallows Tortoise. Tortoise then begins to discomfit Cow by drumming and singing nasally in his belly and, when Cow gets to Ogiso, the *Oba*, to report his strange experience, Tortoise drums and sings, calling on Ogiso to kill Cow. Cow is killed and dissected. Tortoise is set free, and carries home the lion's share of Cow's body as meat. The first single plot ends. A resolution has been reached.

The second plot begins when Tortoise visits Dog and narrates his exploits with relish. Dog feigns being pressed to urinate and asks Tortoise to wait in his (Dog's) sitting room. As soon as Dog is out of Tortoise's sight, he races to Tortoise's kitchen, devours his cherished cow meat, defecates in his pot, and returns to him. Shortly after, Tortoise leaves Dog's home to discover, to his great chagrin, that he has been tricked. He then feigns illness and sends for Dog, his 'friend', to come and help him set an iron trap. Dog comes. But as he bends low over the trap, Tortoise repeatedly drives a red-hot iron perforator into Dog's anus. When Dog regains balance, he counter-attacks Tortoise with an iron hammer, which badly cracks Tortoise's hitherto smooth shell. Another resolution has been reached, thus ending the second single plot.

The second sub-kind of the double plot, which is a juxtaposition of two contrasting single plots, is also exemplified by an Ika folktale, 'Ejimuchemebi'. In it, Ejimuchemebi and Ejimucheosaebi are commissioned by the Council of Elders of their town to preserve for use, in five weeks time, a quantity of salt which the elders divide equally between the two young men. The motivation of the two young men is service to their home town, but their methods turn out to be different. Ejimuchemebi ties up his share of the salt and without consulting anyone, climbs up a palm tree and hides the parcel in the fronds. Ejimucheosaebi goes to an old woman to seek advice. He is advised to tie up his own share of the salt and hang it above the fire-place. He does so. On the appointed day, Ejimucheosaebi presents his share of the salt hard and dry; Ejimuchemebi cannot find his own, for the rains have washed it all away. At the end of the tale, therefore, Ejimucheosaebi is honoured while Ejimuchemebi is in disgrace. In having two simultaneous progressions of events, this sub-kind of the double plot resembles the compound plot, but neither its characters nor their circumstances or eventual fortunes are united as in *The Tempest*.

The third kind of plot in the African folktale is what we have called the multiple plot. It is a unilinear chain of more than two single plots. As with the double plot, the same motivation or different motivations may be found at the beginning of each single plot. Again, apart from motivation, setting, or a major character, or a combination of these may bind the plots together.

'The Twins' in *Fourteen Hundred Cowries* is an example of a multiple-plot folktale. It has four 'well-constructed plots', which, in Aristotle's words 'must have a beginning, a middle and an end' as well as 'a certain length . . . which can be easily embraced by the memory'.[11] These are the Taiwo-monster plot (pp. 29–31), the Taiwo-army general plot (pp. 31–4), the Taiwo-monster's mother plot (pp. 35–7) and the Kehinde-monster's mother plot (pp. 37–41). Other examples of the multiple-plot folktale are 'The Creation' in *Myths and Legends*, which Knappert actually divides into seven parts, each of which could be said to contain a plot; the Ijaw saga published in J.P. Clark's *The Ozidi Saga*; and three out of the sixty Ika folktales studied by the present writer, namely, 'Tortoise and the Farmer' (four chained single plots), 'The Little Boy and his Guinea Fowl' (eight single plots), and 'The Mischievous Little Boy' (three plots). Sometimes, one encounters a tale that has more than two plots but cannot be classified with certainty because some of the plots have been improperly delineated. An example is 'The Orphan Boy and the Magic Twigs' in *Fourteen Hundred Cowries*. On the whole, the multiple-plot folktale is, perhaps, the rarest among African folktales.

Plot Development

The plots of the typical African folktale develop chronologically and with intense clarity. We have observed that a plot begins when a protagonist has been naturally motivated to embark on an enterprise which elicits the main action or conflict. From then on, events come in their natural sequence, through the climax to the anti-climax or resolution; there are neither cutforwards nor flashbacks. This simple progression of the plot of the African folktale does not render it less aesthetically pleasing. Imbedded in the plot is a good measure of suspense and surprise, aesthetic elements which enrich the texture of an ordinarily uncomplicated plot. Let us briefly examine the roles of these elements in the development of plot in the African folktale.

Suspense occurs 'when a decisive action is delayed or when the space of time between an action and its consequence is protracted', while surprise is a sudden and unexpected occurrence which has relevance to events before and after it.[12] In the African folktale, suspense and surprise are often interwoven, although they may also occur separately. In 'The Twins' (already cited), for example, after Taiwo's four pets and sword have been petrified by the old woman's palm wine, Kehinde comes, with his own pets and sword, looking for him. He meets the same old woman, who, again, fetches a large bowl of palm wine. Then we are told.

> Kehinde had practised medicine for a long time and he knew he must be on his guard against this old woman and her palm wine. When Kehinde had refreshed himself, the old woman passed the wine to the animals and the hawk and they all drank to satisfaction. (p. 40)

We are surprised that Kehinde and his pets (in spite of what is stated in the first sentence) still drink the old woman's palm wine. We are, at the same time, thrown into suspense: will they also be petrified?

In 'Omaninja', an Ika folktale, Igbon wanders into the deep forest, as she approaches confinement, since she has no relatives to look after her. She stumbles on a hut. She does not find anyone inside, but, tired of roaming, she decides to sweep the hut clean and stay there. Soon, a strange man, Eferengbukwu, approaches, raving madly at whoever was trespassing in his home. But after the woman has passionately pleaded with him, he agrees to accommodate her. Blindfolded by the man, she later gives birth. She hears the baby cry, but Eferengbukwu takes the child away, puts it in his medicine pot behind the house and returns with a defruited palm bunch, which he places between the woman's legs. This is a surprise. But it is also the beginning of suspense: What will Igbon do? What will the strange man do to her if she protests? What will become of the child? Igbon does not protest for fear of being harmed and she hears nothing more of her child until about three months later when Eferengbukwu hands back to her a well-fed baby boy!

Then Alahin, Ogiso's first wife, snatches the boy from her and throws him into the river. Igbon does not tell her husband. That is another surprise which breeds suspense: Will the boy drown? Will Ogiso, who has been in desperate need of an heir, ever hear of Alahin's atrocity? What will happen to Alahin, if he does? This suspense, which begins before the middle of the tale, lasts until its end.

When suspense occurs singly in the African folktale, it has the usual significance. But when surprise occurs singly, especially at the end of the last of the plots of a double-plot or multiple-plot folktale, it has the effect of a 'twist' and causes one to reflect on the resolution of the preceding plot or plots. Unlike in drama, however, it has relevance only to events before it, since no events come after it in the tale. Yet it usually provides the basis for an explanation of some phenomenon in nature. In 'The Twins', for example,

> Taiwo and Kehinde inquired of their mother's grave, and going to the spot, Kehinde unfastened his loads. 'I have brought along with me the magic liquid we found in the old woman's house, that which I poured over you to bring you back to life. Let us pour it over our mother's grave and see what happens.' . . . Taiwo agreed, and they poured the liquid from one calabash over the grave. Immediately there was a great rumbling and the ground began to move under their feet . . . and the twins moved quickly from the spot as the ground rose. Soon the ground was split asunder and over the spot where their mother's grave had been, there appeared a great rock – Olumo surprise. The rock can be seen at Abeokuta to this day. (pp. 43–4)

In an Ika folktale, 'The Little Boy and his Guinea Fowl', a multiple-plot folktale, the boy satisfactorily barters away his property in seven plots. He begins with the guinea fowl, which his trap had caught and at the end of the seventh plot, he has a line of beads. Then he moves over, in the final plot, to Kpakpaturun, the male earthworm. Kpakpaturun decides to try on the line of beads. He winds it round his neck and goes underground. The little boy sings the song with which he usually demands an exchange for his commodity; Kpakpaturun does not return. That is a surprise. It ends the folktale that has been a chain of eight single plots and there is no question of it being relevant to subsequent events in the tale or of its arousing suspense. But we are told immediately that the event accounts for the 'lines of beads' we find today round the neck of the male earthworm!

Conflict

Conflict may be defined as the struggle that ensues when two contrarily motivated characters or groups of characters strive to achieve certain goals, each through the ruination of the interests of the other. Conflict is manifested, therefore, according to Lajos Egri, in 'attack' and 'counterattack' through words and/or deeds.[13]

One may identify six kinds of conflict in African folktales: verbal, physical, intellectual, intellecto-physical, metaphysical and psychological. Two or more kinds may be found in a folktale depending on its number of single plots. Two kinds of conflict may also develop simultaneously in the same plot or one may develop into another.

Verbal conflict is, of course, one in which words are the only instruments of attack and counter-attack. Physical conflict is prosecuted with the fists or with weapons capable of causing destruction or bodily harm. The intellectual conflict is a battle of wits. The intellecto-physical conflict begins with the wit as the instrument of attack but ends with fists or weapons or other destructive means employed in counter-attack. Metaphysical conflict is attack and counter-attack prosecuted by means of charms or poisons or invisible forces. The last kind, phychological conflict, may be described as a confrontation of a character with himself when his emotion and reason are contrarily motivated. Here are some examples of the kinds of conflict we have described.

There is only verbal conflict in 'The Orphan Girl's Kola Tree', in Ika double-plot tale. A very serviceable orphan girl, while doing all the chores in the home of her mistress, also runs errands for neighbours whenever they need her help. One day, an old woman presents her with a kola nut in return for her services and asks her to plant it. She plants it. As the kola begins to grow, she requires something with which to fence it round so as to prevent domestic animals from trampling on it. Her mistress offers her the neck of her long-since broken and long-cast away earthen pot. The orphan girl gratefully picks up the neck of the broken pot from the bush near the house and uses it to fence her young kola tree. The tree grows bigger until the wide neck of the pot comes to fit it quite closely.

Soon, the kola tree begins to bear *ejije* and *ikpewe*, both costly coral beads. The orphan girl's wealth starts to grow. Being good-natured, she shares her wealth with her mistress. Yet her mistress is so full of envy that she decides to destroy the kola tree. She asks to be given back the neck of her pot, round and unbroken, even though it has become nearly engrafted into the trunk of the tree. The girl points out to her mistress that only the felling of the tree would make possible what she wanted. She therefore pleads with her to forgo the neck of the pot. Her mistress does not budge. Neighbours plead with her also to no avail. Later, the ghost of the orphan's mother advises the orphan to do what her mistress wishes and promises that the kola tree will return to life after it has been felled and the neck of the pot removed. The girl then requests some young men to cut down the tree after which the useless neck of the pot is given back to its owner.

Later, the mistress's only son, an infant, falls ill and an oracle says he will die if a metal ring is not immediately put round his neck, a ring that is perfectly round and without a crack. The orphan girl lends her mistress one such ring and she puts it round her child's neck. The child soon grows to become a huge and powerful young man and the formerly wide ring becomes a mere choker round his neck. The time is ripe for the orphan girl to take revenge on her mistress. She asks that her ring be returned to her, round and without a crack. Her mistress and her solicitors argue and plead in vain. The mistress has her son beheaded and returns the ring to the orphan girl.

In neither of the two plots above is there a physical confrontation between the protagonist and the antagonist. It is significant that the mistress does not fell the kola tree with her own hands and the orphan girl does not physically raise a finger against her mistress's son. In fact, neither of the two overtly suggests the destruction of the other's belonging. There is no clandestine attack as no charms are used. The conflict in each plot is purely verbal.

Examples of physical conflict occur in 'The Jealous Husband', 'The Trapper', 'The King's Daughter' and 'Shamshuni (Samson)', all in *Myths and Legends*, and in 'The Twins', already cited. Intellectual conflict occurs in most animal tales in which the Tortoise or the Hare or the Spider or the Snake is a major character; examples are 'Handy Hare and the Drought' and 'The Baboon and the Tortoise', in *Myths and Legends*.

An example of the intellecto-physical conflict is found in a Kikuyu tale, 'The Hyena, Wakahare, and the Crow' in Finnegan's *Oral Literature in Africa*.[14] The Hyena tricks the hungry Crow into removing the stitches in his anus, which had prevented him from evacuating, by promising Crow a lot of meat from his (Hyena's) belly. When Crow loosens the first stitch, two small pieces of meat, indeed fall on the ground, which the Crow devours greedily. But when he loosens the second stitch, after great effort, 'a burst of white excrement gushed forth with such vehemence, that the poor Crow was cast back ten feet and was buried head and all under a heap of very unpleasant matter'.[15] The Crow then decides to take revenge. When he hears that 'the hyenas had arranged for a great dance in a thicket', he goes there to promise them 'a great quantity of good meat and fat' if they could follow him up to the sky where birds stored their meat. On the appointed day, he tells them:

> 'You must grapple one another by the tail, so as to form a long chain. The first of the chain will hold fast to my tail'. . . At a given sign, the Crow began to fly, lifting the hyenas one by one till they looked like a long black chain waving in the air. (p. 350)

Soon, the hyenas can no longer see anything on earth. Then Crow asks them to let go for a while, that he may readjust his ornaments. The hyenas plead that that would be dangerous. But 'with a sharp jerk he (Crow) turned to the right. The feathers of his tail tore out, and with them the long chain of hyenas.'

Metaphysical conflict is well exemplified by the encounter between Kehinde and the old woman in 'The Twins' and by 'The Tail of Ogiso's Wife', an Ika folktale. In each, there are two levels of action, the superficial and the profound. At the superficial level is pretence of friendship; at the profound level, the battle rages, a battle of *juju* against *juju*.

Psychological conflict seems the least employed in African folktales. Actually, it is fully developed in only one of the folktales known by this writer, 'Dove and Melon Seeds', an Ika folktale. Dove seeks the advice of the oracle on how to achieve longevity for his lineage. He is told to stop eating melon.

On a farm, the following day, he finds plenty of melon seeds in melon fruits that have been cut open for fermentation. A conflict arises between Dove's inner and his outer self. His inner self says, 'I will not eat', but his outer self says, 'I will'. On that day, his inner self wins; Dove merely looks at the melon seeds and does not touch them. On the following day, the tables are turned. It has rained and the melon seeds are glittering like fire flies under Dove's nose. According to the performer of the tale, 'Dove jumped on them (the seeds). He ate; he ate; he ate. Dove straightened up and said, 'Have I died yet?' Dove's outer self's confidence waxes stronger. It wins over his inner self more resoundingly on the third day. But on the fourth day, as Dove is about to begin feasting on the seeds, he falls into a trap, which had been set by the owner of the farm.

Conflict Development

In the African folktale, as in drama, all conflicts are not equally developed. A fully-developed conflict could be represented thus: motivation-attack–countermotivation–counterattack–resolution. This pattern is clear in 'The Hyena, Wakahare and the Crow' discussed earlier. In it, the motivation is to regain convenience; the attack is a trick which results in the Crow being overwhelmed by excrement; the countermotivation is revenge; the counterattack is also a trick, which results in the great fall of the hyenas – the resolution. There is, however, a rising-hurdle pattern of conflict development which may also be found. It is one in which the protagonist is up against natural obstacles which become fiercer and fiercer as the final resolution draws near.

Judging from the folktales here studied, one may find fully developed conflict in about forty per cent of any random collection of African folktales. In some instances, the story is terminated when attack has occurred and there is no opportunity for counterattack, as in 'Mutoro' and 'The Stick' (*Myths and Legends*). In the former, Mutoro, a poor fisherman catches a snake, but the snake regains his freedom by bribing him with a purse full of silver. 'When the sultan heard that Mutoro was now a rich man he came and took the purse from him' (pp. 150–51), and that is the End! This contrasts with 'The Simpleton and the Sultan' in the same collection, in which the sultan seduces and snatches the beautiful wife of the simpleton and the simpleton drums up the whole country to 'war against the sultan', and plunder and set fire to his palace. 'The simple man found his wife and took her home'. In other instances, conflict is developed in one out of a chain of plots or the attack in the first is countered in the second or the third plot in the chain. Tales with undeveloped conflict are generally less aesthetically satisfying than those with fully developed conflict. The audience can notice signs of haste or memory lapse or bad craftsmanship on the part of the story teller.

However, in tales that show off the power of the devout, as in the tales about the prophets in *Myths and Legends* (pp. 35–64), full development of conflict is, perhaps, unnecessary, lest the prophet is discredited! In purely propagandist or heteronomous tales, as in, 'Lion and Mouse' and in some aetiological tales, such as 'How the Sky Went Up', conflict is not even introduced at all. These two folktales are found in several African cultures. In the first, the Lion catches the Mouse and is about to eat him. The latter pleads to be released because of his small size and inability to satisfy the Lion's hunger. The Lion considers the plea and releases the Mouse. Months later, the Lion is caught in a trap. As he thrashes about in pain, the Mouse comes by. He advises the Lion to stop struggling and keep his trapped foot steady. The Mouse then nibbles steadily at the rope that has gripped the foot. He soon cuts the rope and releases the Lion. One good turn deserves another.

'How the Sky Went Up' is about the beginning of time. The sky was low and God allowed people to cut pieces out of it for food, with the injunction not to cook too much at a time and waste it. But a greedy pregnant woman breaks the injunction and the sky moves out of the reach of mankind.

Conclusion

If plot and conflict in African folktales and how they are developed are not exactly what one finds in written literature, it may be partly because the styles and processes of creation and propagation are not the same in the two kinds of literature and partly because the two forms make unequal demands on the memory. The epic aside, the longest folktale is shorter than the novelette. The epics are not usually completely performed in one night just as a novel may not be read to the end in one day. But while the reader of a novel may stop at the middle of an episode or even a paragraph and continue from there the next day, the audience of the epic may not be exactly the same on two successive nights and the part of the epic to be performed the second night may not make sense to the new members of the audience unless it is, in a way, an organic unit of meaning, a complete link in a chain. Even assuming that the audience would be the same, an organic unit would still be needed so that it could be completely enacted and fully grasped by the average memory for one night. Also, children are a major part of this audience.

There are also the mental and physical demands on the performer to meaningfully arrange the incidents and clearly relate them through his own extempore diction and mimesis. Therefore, even the long (non-epic) tales are organised in linked single plots.

Conflict in the African folktale is, ideally, developed the same way as in well written literature: it rises in waves to a climax and ebbs to a resolution. But one single conflict in the folktale is hardly sustained beyond a proportion that is manageable in the circumstances already described. A literary play in performance is, after all, not stopped midway to be continued the following day, although its conflicts are also not organised in such a way that they may be singly detachable.

The African folktale, as art, may, therefore, be judged by its own parameters. The highlights of this paper may point to those parameters, but more work needs to be done to establish them.

NOTES

1. A full discussion of these perspectives may be found in Ruth Finnegan, *Oral Literature in Africa* (London: Oxford University Press, 1972), Chapter 12.
2. For example, Helen Chukwuma, 'Taxonomy of African Oral Literature', paper presented at the 8th International Conference of African Literature and the English Language, University of Calabar, Calabar, 2-5 May 1988, and Sam Ukala, 'Functions of the Folktale: A Case Study of the Ika Folktale', *Ekpoma Journal of Languages and Literary Studies*, 2 (1989).
3. Sam Ukala, 'Transmission of the Folktale by Print: the Question of Authenticity and Reliability' in *Literature and Black Aesthetics*, ed. Ernest Emenyonu (Ibadan: Heinemann, 1990).
4. Aristotle, *Poetics*, in B.F. Dukore, *Dramatic Theory and Criticism: Greeks to Grotowski* (New York: Holt, Rinehart and Winston, 1974): 36.
5. Aristotle: 40.
6. Aristotle: 40.
7. These examples are from drama, not only because the folktale is a performed art, but also because plot is more graphical and palpable in drama than in prose fiction.
8. The Ika are Ibos of Bendel State, Nigeria.
9. F. Abayomi, *Fourteen Hundred Cowries* (Ibadan: Oxford University Press, 1967).
10. J. Knappert, *Myths and Legends of the Swahili* (Nairobi: Heinemann Educational Books, 1970).
11. Aristotle: 38.
12. H.D. Albright, W.P. Halstead and L. Mitchell, *Principles of Theatre Art*, 2nd Edition (Boston: Houghton Mifflin Company, 1968): 27.
13. L. Egri, *The Art of Dramatic Writing* (New York: Simon and Schuster, 1960): 178-9.
14. R. Finnegan, *Oral Literature in Africa* (Nairobi: Oxford University Press, 1976): 347-50.
15. Finnegan: 349.

Oral Echoes in Armah's Short Stories

Ode S. Ogede

Armah's comment on the allegations by Charles Larson,[1] that he modelled *The Beautyful Ones Are Not Yet Born* (1968) and *Fragments* (1970) on the novels of the Irish writer James Joyce, offers a telling indication of the role of oral tradition in his fiction:

> For the benefit of anyone curious to know where I did get the organizing idea for *Fragments* from, it grew out of a conversation with my elder brother concerning the quality of life at home [his native Ghana].[2]

The key concept suggested above is that of conversational narrative, an art form that seeks steadily to keep in touch with the social reality which it mirrors. It can be legitimately stated that the heritage of his elder brother's culture that Armah juxtaposes with the western tradition of James Joyce is the African story-telling tradition because among Armah's Akan, as among some other African groups, the art of story-telling is part of the daily experiences that inevitably influence the individual brought up in the local environment. Armah himself belongs partly in this tradition by virtue of his upbringing. No one who approaches them with a firm grounding in the African oral tradition should fail to notice that, both in his longer fiction and, more particularly, the short stories Armah principally employs the style of a story-teller who regards his role as being that of a performer with a moral to teach, and a lesson to impart.

The sense of having a mission to teach and to analyse issues of public concern is one of the features that, in general, the modern African writer has borrowed from the oral tradition. Like the traditional oral artist, whose works must be rooted in the social reality of his society in order for his lesson to have the resonance and authenticity expected of someone who is the conscience of the nation, Armah fights back the urge to dwell in his stories on a romanticised, numinous world far from the experience of the common people whose ideas, problems and aspirations he explores. So that his six published short stories so far,[3] all bear the mark of his crusade as a cultural nationalist primarily involved in the task of employing traditional story-telling devices in the creation, in a modern context, of a society that is rid of oppression, injustice and chaos, and where all can live in harmony with one another and march forward with some sense of direction. Thus Armah's use of techniques of oral expression to structure his stories demonstrates the commitment of a writer determined to harness the immediacy of impact and the urgency inherent in the short-story medium for the welfare of his society.

To begin to understand the significance of the exercise that Armah is engaged in, we must realise that, traditionally, the short story has been regarded as a most effective vehicle for instruction because it dispenses with the extensive embroidery and ornamentation built into other forms like the novel and the literary drama, while managing to carry equal appeal with these other genres. Whether it is at the occasions of story-telling by the fire-side on moonlit nights in many an African village, or in the modern context of reading in solitude, it is its economy, brevity, directness and charm that make the short story a favourite with those who have neither the leisure nor the patience for the other longer and more involved narrative modes.

The traditional raconteur usually performs before an audience which is a living presence before the artist, with whom the performer establishes a rapport by engaging the audience as both observers and participants in the events enacted. The audience participation and involvement often comes through the group's gestures, instrumental/musical accompaniment, verbal/choral responses or songs.[4] Because the project of adopting an oral text perfectly in the written mode has remained an ideal much desired but yet to be attained, at best what Armah attempts is to incorporate some of the devices of oral expression in his short stories; and for this project, he relies on narrators who create a semblance of direct communication with their audience. The direct address is thus the main vehicle in the author's experimentation with the mode of invented dialogue.

It has been observed that the technique of direct address is most effective, especially when wedded to the first-person narration frequently favoured in traditional contexts because of the latter's suitability to the creation of reader empathy by giving him the illusion of 'undergoing all the protagonist's adventures and sharing with him the revelations brought by his experience'.[5] A modern writer like Armah shows that a similar impact can also be registered through the third-person narrator. Although this phenomenon, which represents Armah's newest and most innovative contribution to the African short-story tradition, can be observed in all his stories, it is most poignantly illustrated in his very first published work of fiction, 'Contact' (1965), and 'Asemka' (1966). In these stories in particular, he evinces the style of presenting third-person narrators who convey an impression of being confronted by an audience in a performance situation.

One other significant point that needs to be borne in mind in discussing these works is that even though he does not succeed in capturing all the nuances of an oral event, yet, how Armah fills this gap is itself interesting. For example, a most commonly lost feature of the oral mode in the stories is the dramatic intensity of the traditional tale usually evoked by ideophones.[6] Armah employs descriptive passages that could in the hands of a less skilful writer be merely redundant but which he uses masterfully to thrust readers straight into the climax of his protagonists' crises. In 'Contact', this device is effective in the sense that in the story, which centres on the predicament of a certain Lowell, a black American who can neither feel at home in white society, to which history has condemned him, nor in Africa, from where he has been severed, through a vividly realised descriptiveness Armah is able to portray the setting of the action realistically and authentically.

It is winter in America, where, Kobina, an African college student, has completed a semester and is left 'feeling wound up, exhausted', as 'though something that had been tied up for a long time was beginning to flow again, demanding contact with things outside of himself' (p. 244). Kobina's desire reflects the mood of others like Lowell, who appear to be people in need of outlets for their suppressed energies.

An evocative and disturbing story, 'Contact' makes no pretence at offering any simplified solutions to the dilemma of blacks in America caught between two antithetical cultures. As the party organised in Lowell's apartment demonstrates, it is impossible to socially bring the races together because effective communication, especially between blacks and whites, is often elusive. And Armah ends his story by ridiculing the view of Lowell who regards rebelliousness of solitary individuals as being sufficient to bring an end to the institutionalised subjugation of blacks, in the same way as he satirises Carin, a white girl whose effort to identify with blacks he presents as an academic exercise that provides the liberal expiation for her racial guilt.

Instead, Armah echoes the didacticism of the oral tradition in 'Contact' and makes a call on black people in America to return to Africa, spiritually and physically. And, although his views in this direction might seem impractical and ridiculous in the light of their running counter to the beliefs of most black Americans at the time (the mood of blacks at the time is summarised by Stokely Carmichael and Charles V. Hamilton who argue in their book *Black Power: The Politics of Liberation in America* that black people 'must create power bases, of strength, from which black people can press to change local or nation-wide patterns of oppression'[7]) yet, Armah demonstrates great courage in being willing to uphold views that were diametrically opposed to ideas that were in the air at the time he wrote the story. To this courage I shall return in a moment, but first will examine the possibility of putting down in writing the echoes of an oral performance in 'Asemka'.

The theme of 'Asemka' is the erosion of traditional values by western vices and, quite appropriately, it is narrated by an old woman who had witnessed the idyllic past being threatened. As a witness to the generational changes taking place, she conveys the sacrilegious story to an audience whose sympathy to her point of view she takes for granted. The narrator lived in a compound with Mr Ainoo, a clerk, and his daughter Essie, and she witnessed the seduction of Essie by Mr Mensah, another new African in the compound. She could have disclosed the illicit affair and presumably prevented Essie's out-of-wedlock pregnancy which results in a serious social stigma, but for the attitude of the 'new people', who were so arrogant and scornful of communal solidarity, humility and respect for elders – qualities that are cherished by Africans like the narrator – that they refused to return even everyday greetings. Thus she too adopts the attitude of the newcomers' indifference to other people's affairs and the pregnancy, which soils Essie's family name and brings shame to all involved in the case, is the price they pay for embracing false values.

The story's opening passage gives the illusion of an oral performance which Armah sustains throughout:

> Mr Ainoo is not a good person. He is not a bad person, but he has too much respect for himself; so he has no respect left for anybody else. Have you ever seen a man who lives in the same house with you, crosses your footsteps wherever he moves, eats food cooked in the same kitchen as your own, stands where you stand to wash himself; have you ever seen a man like that, who lives in the same house with you, but would rather die than greet you even once?
> ('Asemka', p. 28)

The passage employs the traditional technique of 'riddling' that is conventionally most suited to explorations of mystery. The writer creates suspense in the audience by means of lyrically balancing incantatory statements which use parallel structures built on incremental repetition. These confer a sing-song quality to the passage that thrills the audience whom it transports, as it were, in a hypnotic fashion to a land of miracles. The attempt to capture the musical quality of an oral performance in 'Asemka' enhances the sense of the writer's social commitment.

Although he is working with English, a borrowed language and in the written medium, Armah achieves the goal of an oral event with sound effects, by playing on a complex set of rhythms. By focusing the reader's attention on the conflict between traditional African and Western values from the perspective of the unrest caused in a family whose members are caught up in the tension, he makes the experiences described allegorical rather than particular or individualistic.

'Yaw Manu's Charm' (1968) exemplifies the fact that often the style of handing out advice and moral injunctions to the reader in Armah's moralising stories is not as simplistic as it may at first appear. By emphasising the psychological and social consequences of the Western intrusion, the story truly anticipates *Why Are We So Blest?* (1972). Both are classical examples of in depth character studies that rely mostly on methods of introspection. Both deal with the comprehensive way in which Western education implants false standards on Africans and other subject peoples, and the resultant alienation of the victims from their indigenous cultural heritage, their identity crisis or loss of dignity. Whereas in the 1972 novel Armah concentrates on the operation of the system in the metropole – the centre where, in the words of Modin, one of the novel's main characters, 'the crudest forms of manipulation' take place[8] – in 'Yaw Manu's Charm' he specifically looks at the role of the imported structures in their new settings in Africa. In either case, he reaches the same conclusion, that the integrity of the African is perverted by corruption institutuionalised by Western education. Like the novel, 'Yaw Manu's Charm' is an important exploration of 'the effects of neo-colonial psychology'.[9]

Yaw Manu's story begins at the end of his career when, like Achebe's Obi Okonkwo of *No Longer at Ease*,[10] the protagonist is jailed for corruption. The story's retrospective narrative device thus allows Armah, like Achebe in his novel, to select relevant experiences from the protagonist's past and fill in details with comments.

> Now that he is in prison, some people are afraid even to say that they knew Yaw Manu. He has become a leper. That's because he was caught, not because these people shun evil. After all, everybody knows that it is impossible for an honest man to become rich, and yet the rich are respected.
> ('Yaw Manu's Charm', p. 89)

The opening style of heightening suspense derives from oral tradition and effectively suits a raconteur who already knows the end of the story from the outset but has to reserve the choicest detail till the close of his tale. The adoption of an omniscient third-person narrative voice is truly befitting because his intimate knowledge of the debased atmosphere against which the protagonist should be judged contributes to the overall effect he has on the audience. Thus, the narrator loses no time in recounting Manu's life history right from the elementary school where they were classmates. This has the desired effect of establishing his singular compassionate and intimate knowledge of his subject – an attribute that is needed to sustain the credibility of his story.

By disclosing Manu's undoing element as being his everlasting ambition to win 'a big scholarship' one day to study in England, a place that was 'always in his head ... like a disease, eating him and making him live only in the future, far from us all and everything around him' (p. 89), he portrays Manu as a person who was a victim of his circumstances rather than one who was biologically perverted – a figure more acted upon than acting. Notwithstanding that the author indirectly holds the three institutions of the Catholic Church (standing for Christianity in general), domesticated Islam in Africa, and finally the colonial educational system responsible for Manu's corruption, he fails in the story to come up with an open attack on these institutions.

The inability to push the didacticism of the traditional story to its conclusive end in 'Yaw Manu's Charm' establishes Armah as a modern writer being seduced by the conventions of the modern realist story with its bias against the programmatic or neat ending that is a stock feature of the traditional mode. But in this regard, Armah's performance is instructive because it reveals not only the possibilities but also the limitations that accompany the oral work in its transition to a written text. Nonetheless, he remains able to carry over some of the most important textual content of the oral mode into the written form.

One of the attributes of the story-teller that features in Armah's short stories, on which he depends for his effects, is courage, to which I have earlier referred. This is the quality about which at least two critics have remarked with specific reference to the novels, that his writing is 'radical in thought, and frightening in its frank realism';[11] he is 'one of those writers who articulate in bold language what others are too modest or too nice to put in print'.[12] Armah's handling of the theme of race relations in 'Contact' is an example of his great courage. As Archie Mafeje tells us, courage is an essential attribute of the traditional bard, which enables him to combine the roles of a praise singer and that of a critic of his community whose leadership he must warn not to deviate from the customs and traditions of the society.[13] To regard the bard as merely a praise singer or entertainer at the courts of traditional rulers, is to ignore his vital function as the voice of conscience in his community.

If the determination that Armah manifests in his stories eventually does amount to merely an echo of the legendary dauntlessness of the committed oral artist, his inability to completely identify with the condition of the underpaid workers also partly reflects his own class position as a petty-bourgeois intellectual who is unable to strike an effective accord with the working classes. The stories 'An African Fable' (1968) and 'The Offal Kind' (1969), offer a helpful context in which we can assess Armah's commitment to the cause of the down-trodden. He fearlessly exposes the moral depravity of the African bourgeois elites – a class to which he too belongs as a privileged individual – who took over the leadership of their nations from the white overlords and have since independence perpetrated the exploitation of their own people with a ruthless severity that was unknown even during the colonial era. Yet he fails to make the final thrust in the direction of suggesting strategies that could assist the underprivileged people in their struggle to destroy their oppressors. As a work whose allegorical framework anticipated *The Beautyful Ones Are Not Yet Born*, 'An African Fable' similarly turns on the African elite represented by an 'inexperienced warrior' whose quest for leadership, ironically, ends up as an adventure for self-enrichment. But Armah loses the opportunity to use the situation to make a radical call for the destruction of the oppressor. The warrior journeys across Africa, 'down through the lands of the middle where nothing is really desert and still the forest itself is not yet', then into 'the moistness of the forest land itself' in the south (p. 192). In this phallic story, the warrior's inability to resist the human and material resources of the continent suggests the greed of the elite. Like Senghor in 'Black Woman', Armah embodies Africa in the image of a woman, even though he plays down her beauty and reverses the adulatory tone of Senghor's poem in order to underscore the debased and exploited fate of Africa. Within the story's own moralistic design, armed resistance ought to be the logical means by which the exploited majority can end their exploitation and suffering since the story unequivocally shows that the only language the oppressor understands is the language of force, yet, Armah evades this line of reasoning. Thus the ending of 'An African Fable' displays the muted response of a liberal writer who fights shy of endowing his protagonists with the potential to undertake any heroic action to free themselves.

Given Armah's liberal temperament, therefore, the main interest of 'The Offal Kind' is that it enables readers to measure the degree of his success in the imaginative leap he has taken in his attempt to grapple with the emotional suffering that typifies the lives of ordinary people. In the story, a young girl, Araba, is taken from her mother by a powerful town lady to serve her: 'she was going to be the lady's household help, and if she was good and learned everything there was to learn, she would perhaps be a lady herself one day, perhaps' (p. 79). This theme of exploitation of househelps focuses on a common feature of everyday reality in post-colonial Africa and is also the theme of Achebe's story, 'Vengeful Creditors'.[14]

What makes Armah's story interesting is his peculiar use of oral tradition in his intent to give voice to Araba's suffering. Whereas Achebe focuses in his story on the consequences of the effort by Veronica, his ten-year-old protagonist, to make her master and mistress pay for betraying their promise to send her to school after serving them well, Armah stresses Araba's consequent debasement. She is overworked, exploited, underfed, and then forced to become a prostitute. As in the oral tale, exaggeration is the main feature in Armah's handling of Araba's story, which helps to sharpen the attack on the social set up, an irresponsible establishment, of whose unjust policies Araba is a victim – a society that legitimises the enslavement of the poor by the rich by denying equal opportunities to the people. Armah's intention is to shock the bourgeois elites with a vision of their immorality as a means of forcing them to reform themselves.

That Armah's approach may not escape the charge of sentimentality, nevertheless, becomes obvious when contrasted with Ousmane's radicalism, for instance, in 'Black Girl',[15] where Ousmane casts a glance at such a problem as Araba's, from a racial perspective and then uses the suffering of his protagonist as a launch pad for his call for the destruction of the system which enshrines inequality. Diouana, an innocent young Senegalese girl who serves a French family in Dakar, is lured by her master and mistress, Mr and Mrs Pourchet, to France, as she wishes to improve her lot there. She is overworked and exposed to severe white racism, thus confirming the fears of Tive Correa, an old black sailor who had warned her against going abroad. Like Armah, Ousmane uses the same technical devices of oral expression such as repetition, the fabular mode and exaggeration, which Ousmane successfully blends with a burning search for poetic justice. Not so Armah, who seeks equitable distribution of the national wealth but avoids calling outrightly for a revolution in the orthodox Marxist sense as the best means to bring about egalitarianism.

The foregoing leads to the observation that in Armah's handling of the short-story form his effects are in the aesthetic rather than the political terrain. Armah's stories give pleasure and delight because of his linguistic skill which presents, with humour, a haunting vision of human suffering. This is a quality which the traditional oral narrator uses to hold the attention of his participating audience and which, in the face of tragic suffering, might give the impression of brutality in the artist.

Part of the charm of Armah's stories is that they combine the roles of instruction and entertainment. The combination of fun and education may be carried through caricature as in 'Contact', or by morbid humour as in the sexual licentiousness, gluttony and lechery of the elites in 'Asemka' and 'An African Fable'. It may also be served by a merciless lampooning, as in the use of the grotesque in 'Yaw Manu's Charm'. In every case, the purpose of the humour is to rivet attention while instructing the reader.

'Halfway to Nirvana' (1984) stands as the culmination of Armah's stride towards capturing the flavour of an oral tale using the short-story form that appears to revel in poking fun at human evil. A crusty story, which employs clear symbolism, dramatic techniques and satire to explore the deepening hypocrisy of the ruling elites in Africa, it is narrated by a participant narrator, a journalist who works for a magazine called *Sic*. The political and social situation described is totally decadent, and the story achieves a tone of verisimilitude that each of the previous stories has vainly attempted to achieve. The narrator attends a conference organised to combat drought in Africa. Drought is the symbol of neo-colonial domination of Africa. She meets Christian Mohamed Tumbo, Africa's representative in the Anti-Drought Organisation, who symbolises Africa's political leaders of all religious and ideological persuasions. But his name can also be seen as an indirect reference to Oliver Tambo, leader of the African National Congress of South Africa, and thus to the leadership of the liberation movements in Africa.

In his portrayal of Tumbo, nonetheless, Armah achieves a rare feat of compassionate study that balances satire with humanity. Tumbo emerges as an evil but attractive leader who, like Chief Nanga of Achebe's *A Man of The People*, shamelessly concedes that he is in politics for his selfish interests. Tumbo may nod off during discussions at conferences, and on waking up, assent to decisions reached which he does not even understand, but his is a case of a personality destroyed by a decadent social order. The implied message, certainly, is that Tumbo and the narrator are products of a society which has reduced life to mere sensual satisfaction as individuals await their chance to join the elite in defrauding the nation. Thus, at the end of each conference session, Tumbo can be seen 'far ahead of others; bounding joyfully toward the cocktail bar, a manic spirit unchained' (p. 1947). Tumbo comes from a poverty-striken background which he hates to return to. He was for fifteen years a poorly paid geography teacher in a secondary school in a village. Although he liked the job at first, growing materialism in the country eroded his integrity. He watched his students over the years acquire degrees and money, and make other material advances which caused him to lose his position of respect among the villagers. The lack of a degree stood between him and a job at the Nirvana, but through contacts, he got the job with the Anti-Drought Organisation and all his problems were over. He settled his debts and now owns 'two villas, two embassy residences, rent paid a year in advance' (p. 1948). He owns the building in which he lives but the government rents it for him. Most of the year he lives abroad on a government allowance, while his salary continues to be paid into his bank account at home. Christian Mohamed Tumbo wants the drought to continue indefinitely so that he can keep his lucrative job. Thus 'Halfway to Nirvana' ends as a most subtle investigation of the temptations of power and pours scorn on its corrupting influences.

What has been demonstrated in this brief study is that Armah's short stories test the possibilities of adapting the devices of oral art to the written medium. Its many limitations notwithstanding, his attempt adds richness and vitality to modern African literature. Some of the social ills treated in the stories, like sexual promiscuity among unmarried people, prostitution, petty theft and general moral bankruptcy are grave problems that threaten the very foundations of African societies. The stories are interesting not only because their topics of discussion are timely, but also because the writer shows skill in, and affectionate dedication to, his craft.

NOTES

1. Larson, *The Emergence of African Fiction* (Bloomington: Indiana University Press, 1972). Other critics have seen more western influences. For instance, although not directly making claims of European influence, Eustace Palmer mentions the similarity of *The Beautyful Ones Are Not Yet Born* to *Everyman* or Bunyan's *Pilgrim's Progress*, in *An Introduction to the African Novel* (London: Heinemann, 1971); Achebe alludes to influences on Armah by Sartre, in 'Africa and her writers', in *Morning Yet on Creation Day: Essays* (London: Heinemann, 1975); Margaret Folarin refers to Plato, in her article in *African Literature Today*, 5 (1975); Arthur Gakwandi refers to Kafka in *The Novel and Contemporary Experience in Africa* (London: Heinemann, 1977); Charles Nnolim sees the ghosts of the Goncourts, Walter Pater, Paul Verlaine and Joseph Conrad, Dante and Dickens, in his essay entitled 'Dialectic as Form: Pejorism in the Novels of Armah', *African Literature Today*, 10 (1979): 207–23; See also Robert Fraser, *The Novels of Armah* (London: Heinemann, 1980). I have discussed this issue of debt and influences in greater detail in the following papers: 'Armah and his Euro-centric Critics', a paper presented to the 7th Conference of the Modern Languages Association of Nigeria (MLN), the University of Nigeria, Nsukka, February, 1989; 'Two Decades of Armah Criticism', *Zast: Zeitschrift fur Afrikastudien*, 7/8 (1990): 41–53, and 'Angled Shots and Reflections: On the Literary Essays of Kwei Armah', *World Literature Today* (Winter 1992, forthcoming).
2. Ayi Kwei Armah, 'Larsony or Fiction as Criticism of Fiction', *Asemka*, 4 (1976): 1–4. Reprinted in *Positive Review* (Ife: 1978): 11–14. My quote is from the Reprint, p. 13.
3. 'Contact', *The New African*, December, 1965: 244–6; 'Asemka', *Okyeame*, 3, 1(1966): 28–30; 'Yaw Manu's Charm', *Atlantic Monthly*, May 1968: 89–95; 'An African Fable', *Presence Africaine*, 68. (1968): 192–6; 'The Offal Kind', *Harper's Magazine*, January 1969: 79–84 and 'Halfway to Nirvana', *West Africa*, 24 September, 1984: 1947–8. My page references to the stories will be indicated parenthetically after quotations in the article.
4. See Ruth Finnegan, *Oral Literature in Africa* (London: Oxford University Press, 1970) and Isidore Okpewho, *The Epic in Africa* (New York: Columbia University Press, 1979).
5. Lynn Altenbernd and Leslie Lewis, *A Handbook for the Study of Fiction* (London: Macmillan, 1969): 63–4.
6. For a discussion on ideophonc in oral narratives see Philip A. Noss, 'Description in Gbaya Literary Art', in *African Folklore*, ed. R. Dorson (Bloomington and London: Indiana University Press, 1972): 73–101, and also his 'Creation and the Gbaya Tale', in *Artist and Audience: African Literature as a Shared Experience*, eds. R. Priebe and T. Hale (Washington, D.C.: Three Continents Press and African Literature Association, 1979): 3–30.
7. Stokely Carmichael and Charles V. Hamilton, *Black Power: The Politics of Liberation in America* (Harmondsworth: Pelican Books, 1967): 63.
8. Ayi Kwei Armah, *Why Are We so Blest?* (London: Heinemann, 1974): 32.
9. Derek Wright, 'The Early Writings of Armah', *Research in African Literatures*, 16, 4 (1985): 491.
10. Chinua Achebe, *No Longer at Ease* (London: Heinemann, 1960).

11. O.R. Dathorne, *African Literature in the 20th Century* (London: Heinemann, 1976): 105.
12. Charles Nnolim: 222-3.
13. Archie Mafeje, 'The Role of the Bard in a Contemporary African Community,' *Journal of African Languages*, 6 (1967): 193-223.
14. Chinua Achebe, 'Vengeful Creditors', in *Girls at War and Other Stories* (London: Heinemann, 1972).
15. Sembene Ousmane, 'Black Girl', in *Modern African Stories*, ed. Charles Larson (London: Collins/Fontana, 1971).

Ayi Kwei Armah's
Two Thousand Seasons:
A Dissent

Derek Wright

However deep one's natural antipathy, as a Western critic, to Armah's fourth book, it would be churlish to deny the grandeur and originality of its design and perverse to approach its daring experimentation with the techniques of African oral narrative from the critical assumptions governing discussion of the European novel. Few novels create deliberately unmemorable characters who are merely functions of a collective will or ramble episodically over vast spans of time in pursuit of racial destinies. Even fewer novels start from the premise that certain groups, nations or races have a monopoly on human virtue whilst others, wholly predictable because helpless before the evil of their own natures, have engrossed all the vices, and then proceed, accordingly, to abandon critical investigation for partisan invective. Armah makes no claim to criticise his 'destroyers' and 'predators' and their African quislings but simply hurls abuse at them, more after the fashion of the Ewe *halo* than that of Western satire. These features are, more often, the stock-in-trade of epic, saga and chronicle, both in the African oral tradition of the griot and in its written European equivalents: namely, those Homeric and Norse marathons which similarly trace the migrations of whole peoples and celebrate the founding of nations and empires, but which also use stock epithets with more ironic discrimination, and with a more novel-like, fair-minded openness to the variety of human experience, than are to be found in *Two Thousand Seasons.*

Armah's self-consciously staged griot-like discourse is concerned to correct the method of narrating African history as well as the history itself. There are, therefore, some significant departures from story-telling traditions. His avowedly anti-elitist standpoint shuns the griot's customary glorification of the matchless deeds of past heroes, rejects the supernatural along with the superhuman, and denies the narrator's single creative personality any domineering proprietorship over the events narrated.[1] Armah's discourse makes communal and egalitarian ideals not only potentially realisable in the contemporary world but so certain to be achieved that the goals can be described as having already been won. His

84

world-view is essentially secular and humanist. His narrative strategy emphasises the griot's self-effacing assumption of a common identity with both the specific audience which his tale is designed to educate and the characters of the tale itself. Thus *Two Thousand Seasons* is not only *about* reciprocity: its technique *enacts* reciprocity between the story-teller, his tale and his listeners.

The plural voice of Armah's newly-Africanised narrative form formally announces its agnostic viewpoint in the opening chapter:

> We have not found that lying trick to our taste, the trick of making up sure knowledge of things possible to think of things possible to wonder about but impossible to know in any such ultimate way. We are not stunted in spirit, we are not Europeans . . . What we do not know we do not claim to know.[2]

In the first two novels the author's scepticism about the differences between the present and an ultimately irretrievable past contributed to an ironic and pessimistic vision. In *Two Thousand Seasons*, however, he capitalises on the uncertainty of the past and turns it to positive ends. The narrator does not proceed to a cynical negation of all retrieved 'authenticities', ironically thin though the line may be between the supposed rational ideology of 'the Way' and its rivals, those sentimental mystifications and nostalgic hankerings for unreal pasts which are presented as betrayals of the Way's essential aims. His didactic purpose is to cure an errant Africa of its diseased distrust in its own indigenous forms and values, not to reproduce the exact historical origins and developments of those forms and values. It is accompanied by an awareness that the communal memory drawn upon by the 'remembrances' of oral narrative is no more unreliable than recorded history, especially when the written record is a European one coloured by colonial prejudices, and that a starkly monochromatic portrait of white devilry and black victimisation is at least compatible with Africa's narrow experience of the white man as slaver and coloniser, as material and spiritual destroyer. The dogma of the Way works from the premise that one made-up ethno-centred history, serving one set of ideological needs, is as good as or better than another one which serves different and alien needs. *Two Thousand Seasons*, as Soyinka has observed,[3] stands in the same relation to the work of black ethnologists and historians such as Cheikh Anta Diop and Chancellor Williams as Rider Haggard and Conrad do to the Eurocentric ethnology of Western scholarship. The Prologue's rhetoric of fragmentation and dismemberment issues a reminder that it is the fragmented part of Africa's history – the colonial period which cut the continent off from its past – that, until recently, has alone constituted 'African history' in Western study. Of course, the past is not a total void into which any fiction may be projected. There is a bedrock of verifiable fact to provide yardsticks for authenticity and even Armah's highly postulative, theoretical history, though less concerned with the last than with promise for the future, retains a strong attachment to historical, time-bound reality. The griot's didactic purposes may, however, license historical inaccuracies such as the notions, in *Two Thousand Seasons*, that kings, classes, private property and even adult genesis-fables were all foreign importations (pp. 61, 64, 82, 95, 96), and African hunting skills merely defensive (p. 14). The poet-historian of the African oral tradition is, if only by way of compensation, as entitled to his vagaries of chronology and causation as the Western historian is to his. Armah's story-teller, for example, mixes anticipation and retrospection so freely as to leave less than clear the accounts of those indigenous disruptions of 'Reciprocity' which appear to pre-date the Arab invasions and of the odd infiltration of the fleeing community by the twisted values of its tormentors.

Armah's innovative, pseudo-oral narrative is, of course, a simulated exercise, a literary affectation. It is rendered in English, not in Akan or Kiswahili, and, since communal readings of novels written in English are rare in Africa, the traditional communal intimacy between the artist and his audience is here a mere fiction of the plural voice. *Two Thousand Seasons* is the kind of 'novel' that a griot would have written if he had had access to literary form. In it Armah artificially resolves the problems of the contemporary African artist by setting his tale in an indeterminate past when the artist was not yet alienated from his society but still immersed in a collective ethos, and then using the griot's voice for the vicarious advocation of communal commitment and popular revolution in a period when this is no longer the case. Since the book's message is aimed not at a traditional audience, however, but at those anglicised Africans who have ventured furthest from what Armah considers to be Africa's true self, there is no necessary inconsistency between its form and its initial African publication. Neither does it matter much that the narrative, in its ideological urgency, draws not upon local tribal memories of a specific community but upon the hypothetical race-memory of a fictitious pan-African brotherhood whose names are taken from all parts of the continent: the migrations of the People of the Way suggest the legendary origins of the Akan of Ghana in the medieval Sudanic kingdom of the same name, whilst their acephalous communalism seems to have more to do with the Igbo than the monarchical Akan and the concept of 'Reciprocity' would appear, in the light of the book's Tanzanian genesis, to owe something to the ethics of Tanzanian tribal cultures utilised by Nyerere's *Ujamaa*.[4]

The basic problems created by *Two Thousand Seasons* are formal, aesthetic ones. The oral tale is designed to be said, not read – to be declaimed, not decoded – and its greatest strengths seldom survive its transposition to written form. In Armah's imitative version, oral in conception but literary in expression, the passage between forms is not helped by an erratic and unhappy assortment of styles, ranging from the oracular and invocatory to the popular and idiomatically American: the harem women effect 'the discombobulation of the askaris' (p. 31) and the two mad fugitives from the Arab 'predators' have to be kept 'from trying more homicide' (p. 47). Armah strains to reproduce an illusion of orality and, specifically, of vatic utterance through a formidable battery of rhetorical questions, lamentations, frenzied alliteration – 'This is no hurried hustle hot with sweaty anticipation' (p. 158) – and portentous-sounding adjectivally-launched inversions: 'Painful was the groping after lost reciprocity. Fertile had been the rule of women . . .' (p. 26). The attempt frequently overreaches itself, however, and produces a lugubrious, almost self-parodying rhetoric which is at home in neither the oral nor the literary form. Traditionally, oral narrative edits itself by recantation and cancellation, never by omission – once something has been said, it exists ineradicably – and is apt to convey emphasis quantitatively rather than qualitatively: by the frequency rather than the manner of expression. This failure in economy, translated into written form, leads inevitably to rhetorical redundancies and to what, in novelistic terms, is some of Armah's most unreadable writing. Here is the Way's crude codification of the subtle phenomenology of perception which, in the first novel, aligns sensory and synchronic continuums with group-consciousness:

> The disease of death, the white road, is also unconnected sight, the fractured vision that sees only the immediate present, that follows only present gain and separates the present from the future, shutting each passing day in its own hustling greed.
> The disease of death, the white road, is also unconnected hearing, the shattered hearing that listens only to today's brazen cacophony, takes direction from that alone and stays deaf to the soft voices of those yet unborn.
> The disease of death, the white road, is also unconnected thinking, the broken reason that thinks only of the immediate paths to the moment's release, that takes no care to connect the present with past events, the present with future necessity. (p. 8)

The point laboured here, which is more about time than perception or community, is not really given threefold expression but is monotonously restated in the same form without any regard for the chosen vehicles. No attempt is made to draw upon the peculiar attributes of sight, hearing and thought, which might just as well have been taste, touch and smell. This lustreless demagogic jargon – 'our way, the way', 'the destruction of destruction', 'the unconnected consciousness' – is at its most stark in the formulation of the Law according to the Way, the ten commandments handed down to Isanusi:

> Our way is reciprocity. The way is wholeness. Our way knows no oppression. The way destroys oppression. Our way is hospitable to guests. The way repels destroyers. Our way produces before it consumes. The way produces far more than it consumes. Our way creates. The way destroys only destruction. (p. 39)

The scriptural chant suffers from a kind of hermetic banality, a rhetorical stutter which repeats without revealing and exhorts without enlightening.

Whatever case can be made for the 'historic inevitability' of this kind of writing[5] and whatever its source and ultimate aim, the spectacle of Ghana's major prose stylist wilfully impoverishing his vocabulary by reducing it to the restricted code of a less demanding narrative form is not a happy one. Only in the Prologue are Armah's poetic powers really at full stretch. The interminable and maddening repetition of the Way's sacred trinity of neologisms – 'Reciprocity', 'Connectedness' and 'Creation' – is accompanied by so little explication of what they involve practically as a lived social pattern that they eventually become lifeless verbal tags, self-enclosed abstractions which fail to translate into anything beyond themselves (Armah has more success with 'Inspiration' and 'Manipulation' in *The Healers*). Here is a typical set-piece of rhetoric, following Sobo's freeing of the slaves:

> Ludicrous is the freedom of the slave unchained in his single body if his mind remains a cut-off individual mind, not a living piece of our common mind, our common soul . . .
>
> Sobo was free of the chains holding us, of the traps we were still in. What meaning could his single freedom have had had it been the individual freedom of the unconnected soul? What could we, trapped below, have known of his thoughts, of his intentions and of his actions had he been merely an individual captive singly freed? How then could we have escaped the stupidity of the unconnected viewpoint, each forever petrified in his separate situation, each hardened in her cut-off condition?
>
> . . . How infinitely stupefying the prison of the single, unconnected viewpoint, station of the cut-off vision . . . Such individual action can find no sense until there is again that higher connectedness that links each agent to the group. Then the single person is no cut-off thing but an extension of the living group, the single will but a piece of the group's active will, each mind a part of a larger common mind. Then each eye inspires itself with visions springing from group need, the ear is open to sounds beneficial to the listening group, the limbs move and the hands act in unbroken connection with the group. . . . That is how in the end we came to know what Sobo saw, where he went and what he did there even before his single freedom burst into the fruit of greater liberation. (pp. 133–4)

These are extracts from a much longer tirade which rants *ad nauseam* about the 'connectedness of minds' over a number of pages, and the rhetoric is, in its dramatic context, mainly mystification. Although Sobo uses his skills for the common cause, the captives are freed by his individual enterprise, by a superior personal initiative which does not emanate from the group-mind but separates him from it – an irony which pinpoints the tension between Armah's naturally elitist turn of mind and his socialist commitments. Moreover, the group comes to know what Sobo thinks and intends because, in the dialogue preceding the rhetoric, he tells them: their communication is the perfectly commonplace connectedness of words, not the result of some mystical collective telepathy. The false arguments aside, the depiction of mass-mentalities, though it produces rousing racial propaganda, makes dull, unengaging fiction. The superlative beauty of Anoa and Idawa may have some representational value in the collective consciousness but, as characters, they are negritudinous abstractions, not human beings:

> She [Anoa] was slender as a fale stalk, and suppler. From her forehead to her feet her body was of deep, even blackness that could cause the chance looker to wonder how it was that even the surface of a person's skin could speak of depths. (p. 15)

> Idawa's surface beauty, perfect as it was, was nothing beside her other, profounder beauties: the beauty of her heart, the way she was with people, the way she was with everything she came in contact with; and the beauty of her mind, the clarity with which she moved past the lying surfaces people held in front of themselves, past the lying surfaces of the things of this world set against our way, to reach judgements holding to essences, free from the superfices. (p. 70)

The stylistic failings are not the only ones. The literally black-and-white moral judgements, the pasteboard characterisation's crude differentiation of codes of conduct and the total absence of dramatic tension reduce the episodes of the raid on the castle at Poano and the destruction of the slave-ships to the level of a Boy's Own adventure yarn. At times Armah appears to be writing a kind of African 'Western': 'From an alari branch Kenia placed just one bullet dead between the second would-be killer's eyes' (p. 190).

The Healers is a more balanced and better-written book. Tonally, the solemn racial vituperation of the fourth novel has been diluted to sardonic scorn, though the portraits of Glover and Wolsey are attended by the same gloating self-congratulation, and the book's wealth of circumstantial period-detail does manage to give it the feel of lived history. Nevertheless, Densu's saintly boy-scout heroism, priggish virtue and superman-virtuosity are still uncomfortably close to the physically and ideologically flawless, beautiful creatures of the Way. It is still, as Lindfors maintains, juvenile comic-strip history.[6] Perhaps, as Fraser has argued,[7] the true test of this kind of writing should be its polemical persuasiveness and active efficacy, not its artistic merit, but it is hard for the Western critic to believe that these are not bound up with one another and that persuasion does not rely on competent craftsmanship.

Armah's histories are a therapeutic exorcism, at both the private and public levels. On the level of private penance, the alienated individuals of the early novels are implicitly reproved and outgrown in the harsh treatment of Dovi – 'The selfish desire of the cut-off spirit was so strong in him' (p. 183) – and the selfless sacrifice of Abena: 'There is no self to save apart from all of us. What would I have done with my life, alone, like a beast of prey?' (p. 111). At the public level the therapy is twofold. Firstly, the systematic direction of hatred at Arab and European whites exorcises the sensations of helplessness induced by colonialism and clears the air of negative feeling so that the work of construction may begin: it is a catharsis which prepares the mind for the creation of radical alternatives to the societies left by the imperialists. Secondly, the 'destruction' which the whites inflict and which, to the narrator's delirious glee, they eventually draw upon themselves, provides the relief for the oppositional, mainly negative definition of the Way. Whatever the Way is in itself – and there are times when it seems no more than a convenience category for lost virtues – it is initially everything that 'destruction' is not: 'We are not a people to nurture kings and courtiers . . . We are not a trading people' (pp. 95, 98). 'Leave the destroyers' spokesmen to cast contemptuous despair abroad. That is not our vocation. That will not be our utterance' (p. xvii). The Way, forgotten and not yet rediscovered, is essentially an unknown quantity. Almost everything that happens in *Two Thousand Seasons* is a deviation from the Way insofar as it is not engendered by any major weaknesses inherent in the Way itself, and the retention of the mystery enables the author to blame all the evils that befall it on outside forces. Armah has anticipated the problem of definition in his early essay on African socialism:

> Negative, anti-colonial feeling is relatively easy to come by. At any rate it does not demand any genius. The development of positive programmes and ideologies is a much more difficult proposition.[8]

In practice, this means that the rather drab and joyless communalism which the novelist, with at least part of his mind, wants to believe was the indigenous African way of life emerges as something that is more non-European, and anti-European, than specifically and recognisably African. In fact, certain features, such as the total rejection of family and kin urged upon Dovi and Araba Jesiwa in the name of a higher ideal and the over-riding of territorial instincts by abstract ideological loyalties, would appear to be highly 'un-African', in the sense used by Achebe in his castigation of Armah. Here, as in the early novels, Armah is concerned to question received ideas about 'authentic' traditional values but without putting anything positive in their place.

The continuities with the early novels should not be lost sight of. The growing tendency to blame all Africa's woes upon the West, most pronounced in *Why Are We So Blest?*, stiffens into an explicit racism which, in *Two Thousand Seasons*, presents whites as pathologically evil: 'The white abomination: violence in its pure state, hatred unmixed', runs one of the book's undigested Fanonisms (p. 87). The archetype for the money-making, debased rites of the first two novels is to be found in the slave-king Koranche's ultimate ritual perversion of initiation ceremonies into the bitter rite of middle passage. In the light of the new orthodoxies of the Way, however, the continuities tend to take a corrective form. In the more artificial device of the pluralised narrator who is not localised in place or time, the somewhat contrived notation of communal suffering in the early books – the interchanging narrators at the fulcrum of the first novel, the village in *Fragments* whose name means 'this is everywhere' – finds its culminating and most satisfying expression. Armah's familiar drugged, turgid prose evokes the usual circular notion of time, but with the difference that the circularity now takes the pattern of a progressive return, not entrapment in a cycle of futile repetitions. The recurring colonialisms of contemporary Africa become, on the larger canvas of *Two Thousand Seasons*, temporary aberrations in a wider 'cycle of regeneration' (p. 2), which is destined to carry the continent back to indigenous roots. The 'circle of regeneration' is momentarily 'burst with the invading line of destruction' (p. 154), but this 'white road' of linear fragmentation (roads are always destructive in Armah's novels) proves finally to be merely part of an immense curve on the circular 'path' of the developing Way. The completion of the cycle and the return to unitary beginnings is achieved, however, only by rewriting history. Armah does not so much record history as correct and re-invent it. The successful slave rebellion in *Two Thousand Seasons* is history as it might and should have been, and as it would and will be once the conditions of the Way are adhered to. At the contrived conclusion of *The Healers* the historical wheel is brought to a figurative full circle by the enforced regathering of the black peoples of the world in white captivity. The reality of that captivity and the persistence of the askaris in the work of the whites make the wishful speculations of Ama Nkroma at the closing dance less than convincing:

> It's a new dance all right . . . and it's grotesque. But look at all the black people the whites have brought here. Here we healers have been wondering about ways to bring our people together again. And the whites want ways to drive us further apart. Does it not amuse you, that in their wish to drive us apart the whites are actually bringing us work for the future? Look![9]

The horror of isolation which dogs the careers of the man, Baako and Modin – 'Nothing destroys the soul like its aloneness' runs the departure libation in *Fragments*[10] – is no less marked in the histories. Indeed, it is the main impetus behind the doctrine of the Way. But this horror is now contained and overcome. The ideal society of Densu's dream and the egalitarian mini-Utopias erected around Isanusi's 'Way' and Damfo's 'Inspiration' are essentially no less hypothetical and no more historical than Teacher's dream-past and Modin's *maji*. In each of these visions destruction and alienation are the preserve of the present whilst harmonious fulfilment belongs to the past. But in the early novels the vision is the subject of considerable irony whereas in the later ones it is upheld and celebrated, a trend which brings Armah's writing career to an ironic full circle. The concepts of 'Reciprocity' and 'Connectedness' and the ideal of an egalitarian non-ethnic African fraternity – a fiction which flies in the face of tribal, social and national divisions – are, finally, not very far from the decadent myths of Pan-Africanism and the African Personality derided in the author's first polemical essay. In the terms of that essay, the socialism of the Way is 'Utopian', not 'Scientific'; a wish-fulfilment, not a rational ideology. The germ of the later works' more positive outlook is also present, however:

> First, an analysis of the socialist tradition itself as a mytho-poetic system. The greatest source of power and influence available to the socialist tradition is its acceptance and imaginative use of the archetypal dream of total liberation, the end of all conflict and injustice . . . the thorough-going negation of the repressive facts of real life.[11]

The socialisms of the fifth grove and the healing enclaves are, self-consciously, reality-negating mytho-poetic systems. They are not experienced life-forms to be retained or restored but ideal projections that must be believed in to be created. Their ethical manifestos belong to a higher, speculative order of reality and provide a frame of reference from which the prevailing destruction in the existing reality can be condemned and surmounted. Armah, as griot-like activist, joins in the struggle between creation and destruction depicted in his tale and paradoxically validates his new models for progress by inventing an ancestry for them, thus urging the creation of what does not yet exist by insisting that it has always existed. These two orders of reality – the actual and the postulative – are evident in the naming of the characters in *Two Thousand Seasons*. The rogues' gallery boasts names and accompanying deeds which refer, directly or satirically, to historical personages – Kamuzu to Hastings Kamuzu Banda of modern Malawi, Koranche to the Portuguese-controlled puppet Kwamina Ansa, 'the Golden' to Mansa Musa I of ancient Mali whilst those who serve in the struggle for African freedom – Dedan Kimathi, Irele, Soyinka – are merely items in a list of names. Projected pan-African virtues are thus vaguely opposed to specific historical villainy.

One marked and perhaps surprising continuity between the earlier and later novels lies in Armah's fundamentally elitist outlook. The supermen and superwomen skills which give the fifth-grove guerrillas and the initiate-healers an equality with one another render them superior in every way to the community at large. Armah's adoption of a communal narrative voice and promulgation of group-values do not successfully disguise the continuing polarisation of his characters into benighted multitudes ruled by imbecile potentates and isolated sages and hermits banished, with their impotent wisdom, to the fringes of society. Isanusi's twenty and Damfo's solitary disciples are closer to the communal heart of their societies than the Western-educated intellectuals of the previous books but their literary precursors are, nevertheless, Teacher's wee-group and Ocran's artist-protégés. Densu and Anan, like Baako and Modin before them, are natural winners and champions in any meritocracy but they choose, like their forerunners, to opt out of an unfair competition; they are all individual achievers who decide to abdicate from their superior talents before they can be misused by corrupt powers. The radio song in the first novel addresses itself to these exiled, fragmented fellowships: 'A few people are seeing things and saying them', Teacher responds.[12] In *Two Thousand Seasons* the 'We' of the text identifies not with the masses, except insofar as they are included in the spirit of the community and the race, but, most immediately, with the same superior few, the responsible intellectual elite which acts as the society's conscience:

> But among us the truly empathic have been few since the beginning of our exile from the way. Among a people hustling into doom the feelingless are kings, and the thoughtless always follow kings ... It was not their habit to see through his [Koranche's] protective social pomp and call it empty. And the few whose hearing, whose vision could penetrate its hollowness could not shout loud enough to be heard against the general noise of acquiescence. (pp. 63, 71)

The familiar opposition of these like minds and kindred spirits to an errant mass-mentality is established on the first page of the Prologue: 'You hearers, seers, imaginers, thinkers, rememberers, you prophets called to communicate truths of the living way to a people fascinated unto death ...' (p. xi). The extra-sensory, almost telepathic powers of these 'seers' and 'hearers' are also enjoyed by the 'keen, uncanny eyes and ears' of the 'lunatic seers' who, in the first novel's famous staircase passage,[13] apprehend the rot of contemporary history denied to the merely 'beholding eye' of ordinary mortal sight. Only the 'watching eyes' and 'listening ears' of these enlightened few are alert to the elusive ambivalences of the Way: its constancy of purpose and changing methods of execution and defence, its dynamism – 'We are not a people of stagnant waters. We are of the moving stream' (p. 192) – and its ability to remain unaffected by changing environmental influences and political developments during migrations from deserts to grasslands and forests. The Way to which the few act as spiritual guardians is never the code of the community, which is always heedless of or opposed to it and which, in its advancement towards the status-seeking materialism of Armah's modern Ghana, isolates integrity and intelligence with such ease that the validity of a responsible communal ethic and narrative-view is constantly undermined.

Also seminal to Armah's thought is the division between brute power and persecuted intelligence, idiot-kings and wise philosophers who, in one way or another, are always excluded from power. Here are Koranche's thoughts on the conflict:

> Now life became clear again in his mind: a conflict between the unjustly
> intelligent, the experts with their skill and their intelligence on the one hand,
> and on the other hand those born mediocre, those born inferior through no
> fault of their own, the hollow ones, the stupid ones, the uncreative ones. Lucky
> arrangement indeed, that power in the present world was placed at the dis-
> posal of the latter ... Lucky chance for kings, that power was pitted against
> intelligence. Lucky chance, that talent was suppressible by power. (pp. 73–4)

'Our chiefs, our leaders,' Juma confirms the cartoon-contrasts, 'they have
bellies and they have tongues. Minds they do not have' (p. 146). Dictators
exist by the apathetic permission of their intellectual superiors. 'You have
a fullness you need to bring out', Ocran tells Baako. 'It's not an emptiness
you need to cover up with things.'[14] The motif has re-surfaced, predict-
ably, in everything Armah has written since. Solo speaks of Westernised
Africans being lured towards 'shiny things to waste lonely, useless time
with.'[15] Koranche searches 'in vain for ways to run from his inner emptiness' and cultivates 'external pomp sufficient to cover him in the eyes of
the world, and therefore in his own' (p. 71), whilst his courtiers 'crave
things to eke out their beings, things to fill holes in their spirits' (p. 202).
Koranche is the historical prototype for Koomson and the Principal Secre-
taries. The freedom-fighters and healers are now the collective carriers
of the burden of corrupt leadership, the dead weight of parasitical power
vividly characterised in the 'ostentatious cripples'. Armah's basic vision
has not changed very much. But some of the paradigms and metaphors,
like the African ruler who wants only to live in the slave-castle (Kamuzu,
p. 169), are starting to sound stale and tired and the analysis, instead of
being sharpened and deepened by fresh insights, has been shorn of its
detailed complexity.

There are many ways of being African and the 'Africanness' of Armah's
early novels resides chiefly in their ritualistic sub-texts. Dogma and
diatribe, though not without precedent in African literature, are modes of
another and quite different character, and the two historical works built
upon them are, at best, mixed achievements. Their rejection of despair
and rousing call for a halt to the further fragmentation of African society
by the doubtful blessings of Western culture are positive gestures in a new
direction. But some doubt remains about the method and manner by which
the beautiful ones are finally born and the extent to which the histories'
radical line of departure can be convincingly bent into an arc of continuous development from the early novels. The last two books have
been widely hailed by African critics as evolving what promises to be
a major new style for African literature. Significantly, they have not
given birth to any further works by Armah himself. It may be that their
forced conclusions, confidently envisaging victorious struggle and ultimate re-unification, have left nothing to be said or that their author has

run himself into some kind of formal cul-de-sac. Whatever the cause, their composition seems to have brought Armah's literary career to an abrupt and premature dead-end. Although *The Healers* was not published until 1978, it was completed in 1975. Following the frantic production of five novels in only seven years, the ten-year silence surely speaks for itself.

NOTES

1. Isidore Okpewho, 'Myth and Modern Fiction: Armah's *Two Thousand Seasons*', *African Literature Today*, 13 (1983): 4–12.
2. Ayi Kwei Armah, *Two Thousand Seasons* (London: Heinemann, 1979): 3. Further references are taken from this edition and are given in parentheses in the text of the article.
3. Wole Soyinka, *Myth, Literature and the African World* (Cambridge: Cambridge University Press, 1976): 107–8.
4. T. O. Beidelman,'Kaguru Folklore and the Concept of Reciprocity', *Zeitschrift für Ethnologie*, 92 (1967): 74–88.
5. Soyinka: 109.
6. Bernth Lindfors, 'Armah's Histories', *African Literature Today*, 11 (1980): 95.
7. Robert Fraser, *The Novels of Ayi Kwei Armah* (London: Heinemann, 1980): 105.
8. Ayi Kwei Armah, 'African Socialism: Utopian or Scientific?' *Présence Africaine*, 64 (1967): 15.
9. Ayi Kwei Armah, *The Healers* (London: Heinemann, 1979): 309.
10. Ayi Kwei Armah, *Fragments* (London: Heinemann, 1974): 6.
11. Armah, 'African Socialism': 8.
12. Ayi Kwei Armah, *The Beautyful Ones Are Not Yet Born* (1969; reset ed. London: Heinemann, 1975): 52.
13. Armah, *The Beautyful Ones*: 12.
14. Armah, *Fragments*: 275.
15. Ayi Kwei Armah, *Why Are We So Blest?* (London: Heinemann, 1974): 208.

The Folk Roots
of Flora Nwapa's
Early Novels

Chidi Ikonné

The core theme of Flora Nwapa's early novels, *Efuru*[1] and *Idu*[2], is childlessness and its consequent unhappiness. The author's sustained effort in her first novel to explore the Igbo mythology for the roots of the problem, enhances the establishment of *Efuru*, as a whole, in the fertile soil of the Igbo folk. Although the definition of the problem in *Idu* does not go to the extent of relating childlessness to a specific myth as in *Efuru*, its roots are solidly embedded in the dark soil of Igbo folklore.

Both novels are set in a relatively small Igbo village on a lake. Consequently, as is often the case in Igbo land, the lifestyle of the community is, to a great extent, determined by the wishes of the spirit of the lake.[3] Described in both novels as Uhamiri and the Woman of the Lake, this spirit, a sort of nymph, is popularly known among the Igbo as Mammy Water. She is a symbol of beauty; to liken a woman to her means that the woman is beautiful. Thus the beautiful Efuru is said to provoke the suspicion 'that the woman of the lake is her mother' (Ef. 8). Efuru who sees her in her dreams describes her as 'an elegant woman, very beautiful, combing her long black hair with a golden comb' (Ef. 182). She is also very wealthy. This is evidenced not only by her 'golden comb', but also by the fact that she uses very expensive types of fish as fire-wood (Ef. 183). She thus symbolises the best a man would wish to have in life. It is no wonder, therefore, that the great *dibia* Ogwagara in *Idu* wished he was from the lake village so he could marry her (Id. 41). But Uhamiri is no man's wife in the real sense of the word. Not even Okita's; for, although she is supposed to be married to the owner of the Great River, she is not on speaking terms with him (Ef. 253). Consequently, her name must not be mentioned on the Great River, while Okita's name must not be mentioned on the Lake (Ef. 253).

Nevertheless her wishes are binding on all, both men and women. For example, no fishing is allowed on *Orie* day (Ef. 149, 192). White people do not catch any fish because, apart from their noisy boats which disturb the woman of the lake, they do not observe her rules (Ef. 256). She does not, however, punish them as severely as they deserve because she 'is the kindest of women, kinder to strangers than to her own people. She is very understanding' (Ef. 257).

She is more impatient with prostitutes. A born and self-respecting feminist, she does not equate a woman's self-reliance with prostitution. She 'frowns at it, and that's why prostitutes of our town never profit by it' (Id. 39). She does not tolerate any contravention of her ban on prostitution. 'If any of the women ignored the Woman of the Lake she gave them two to three years in which to repent, that is, to come home and get married like any respectable woman' (Id. 120). Failure to do so results in madness as in the case of Obiaku.

A goddess of contradiction, the spinster-wife of Okita who frowns on prostitution and encourages marriage does not promote a happy married life. Thus, in a community where childlessness is almost regarded as a crime, she does not give children to her worshippers whom she otherwise seeks to make happy through excessive beauty and wealth. The implicit scepticism of the question that ends the novel *Efuru* is, therefore, in place: 'Why then did the women worship her?' (Ef. 281).

This obviously compulsive worship is only one of the practices that inform the folksiness of the two novels under study. There are many more – most of them accurate reflections of their models in the society mirrored in the novels. These include, beginning with Efuru, the folk way of preventing mosquitoes with herbs (Ef. 5); the circumcision of young women before childbirth and the institution of *mgbede* or *mgbopo* (confinement to a fattening room) (Ef. 6 & 10ff.); the folk treatment for convulsion (Ef. 13); the folk way of detecting pregnancy by smell (Ef. 28); acquainting a pregnant woman with what she must not eat or do. For example, she must not eat okra. 'Snail is not good also. If she eats snails her baby will have plenty of saliva.' She should 'not go out alone at night. If she must go out, then somebody must go with her and she must carry a small knife. When she is sitting down, nobody must cross her leg' (Ef. 29–30). Others include, to mention only two other folk practices in *Efuru*, borrowing money with one's child – especially a daughter – as a sort of security (Ef. 42)[4] and rubbing pepper into a child's eyes by way of punishment (Ef. 45). Sometimes the pepper is rubbed into the child's genitals if her offence is sexual.

Folk practices are also the mainstay of the action in *Idu*. These range from the folk way of bringing back a wife who has run away from her husband's house, to the folk approach to solving the problem of paternity. For example, although Amarajeme is sterile and knows well that he is not the real father of his wife's son, he evokes (or at least tries to evoke) the folk custom and tradition to support his claim to the ownership of the baby boy: 'Ojiugo had lived in his house eight months ago so the boy must be his boy.

She was still his wife by custom. Any child born while she was his wife was his child' (Id. 130).

Incidentally, the folktale of the king who has ten wives, told by Efuru in a moonlight folktale session (Id. 151–3), illustrates the Igbo ironic attitude towards adultery and the paternity of the child that results from it. The point is that the palm fruit (symbol of sperm) that makes the hated wife, Mmegbudi (or *mkpọrọmasị*) pregnant is extra-marital. And the king knows it, as he has no intimate relationship with a wife he so hates that he makes her live 'in a place where rubbish and ashes were thrown' (Id. 151). Yet he enthusiastically accepts the 'son' he has not fathered and with him the mother, obviously, an adulterous wife. 'The King drove away all the nine wives, took Mmegbudi into the palace, bought clothes seen only in the land of the white people for her and they lived happily in the palace' (Id. 153).

Indeed, the folk practices which form the mainstay of *Idu* also range on one plane from the treatment of poisoning (Id. 136), to the disposal of the body of a person who commits suicide (Id. 146–7) and on a lower plane, to the treatment of dog bite (Id. 58) and head lice (Id. 72).

The portrayal of all these, as indicated earlier, are near perfect reflections of real practices in the society imitated in the novels. Conversely, Nwapa's presentation of the offering of kola-nuts, alligator pepper and home-made gin, by Efuru, to her angry relations and the acceptance of this 'kola' by the latter does not perfectly mirror her object of imitation. In the first place, Efuru's visitors could not have accepted the kola, the fact that the kola-nuts 'were fit only for kings' (Ef. 4) notwithstanding. They had come as ambassadors of war to bring home by force, if necessary, 'their [erring] daughter who had brought so much disgrace to them' (Ef. 4). Therefore to accept kola, that symbol of mutual good-will, trust and clear conscience, from a co-author of their humiliation would be a betrayal of their mission. A comparison of Nwapa's portrayal with an almost similar situation in Chinua Achebe's *Arrow of God* clearly reveals the implausibility of the episode in *Efuru*.

Akukalia leads an Umuaro delegation of war or peace to Okperi, the home of his late mother. His uncle, Uduezue notices his and his companions' mood and knows, thanks to his knowledge of the Igbo societal norms and values, what will be their reaction to his offer of kola to them. He, nevertheless, declares his intention to make it; then ensue the following dialogue and authorial comment:

> 'Do not worry yourself. Perhaps we shall return after our mission. It is a big load on our head, and until we put it down we cannot understand anything we are told.'
>   'I know what it is like. Here is a piece of white clay then. Let me agree with you and leave the kolanut until you return.'
>   But the men declined even to draw lines on the floor with the clay. After that there was nothing else to say. They had rebuffed the token of goodwill between host and guest, their mission must indeed be grave.[5]

For their part, the ambassadors of war from Efuru's home 'enjoyed the drink very much. They finished the bottle and some of them were even tipsy.' Their mention of the object of their mission is only an after-thought. Worse still, it is as oblique and ineffective as it is reassuring to the enemy: ' "We shall go, our daughter", the spokesman said, "You seem to be happy here and we wonder why your father wants us to bring you back. We shall tell him what we have seen . . . Tell your husband, he must see your father. Let him not be afraid" ' (Ef. 4).

But this is not all. The manner in which the kola-nuts were broken by Efuru's relations is not an accurate imitation of the folk practice in Nwapa's model community. Under normal circumstances, that is, granting that Efuru's relations have no cause to reject the gift, the two kola-nuts would not have been broken and both eaten there and then. The messengers would have returned home with one of the kola-nuts unbroken to show it to their principals. Ọjị ruo ụlọ o kwuo ebe o si bịa (when a kola-nut reaches home it tells where it comes from) says an Igbo proverb.

This recognition of the apparent failure to adhere to the norm does not in any way constitute a condemnation of Nwapa's portrayal. It is possible that she approaches the practice, as she does, in the interest of her art. After all, hers is a novel and not a socio-anthropological study.

In any case, she manifests this right to choose and modify situations which she wants to portray in her novels in her presentation of the folk speech. For example, Nwapa does not always give the exact rendering of Igbo proverbs. A comparison of the following rendering of proverbs by Nwapa with their original Igbo versions will make the point clearer:

Nwapa's Version	Original Igbo Version	Translation of the Original Igbo Version
If an old woman falls twice, we count all she has in her basket (Ef. 14).	*Agadi nwanyị da nda ada abụọ nke atọ aguta ihe o bu n'ụkpa ọnụ.*	If an old woman falls twice, the *third time* we count all she has in her basket.
An elderly person cannot watch a goat entrapped and do nothing (Ef. 67).	*Okonye anaghị anọ n'ụlọ eghu amụọ n'ọbụ.*	'When an adult is in the house the she-goat is not left to suffer the pains of parturition on its tether.' (Chinua Achebe's translation in *Arrow of God*, p. 18).

(*continued*)

Nwapa's Version	Original Igbo Version	Translation of the Original Igbo Version
It is because one has nowhere to touch, that's why one touches the laps (Id. 140).	*Ọ bụ n'ihi a hụghị ebe aga-atụkwasị aka mere ejiri tụkwasị ya n'ikpere.*	It is because one has nowhere to place his/her hand, that's why he/she places them on the knees.

Nevertheless, Nwapa is so determined to make her folk people really sound folk that she does not only make them transfer their native language habits to their pronunciation of such English words as 'glass' which they call 'ganashi' (Ef. 9), but she also actually transliterates their speeches as the following will illustrate:

Igbo Version	Nwapa's Transliteration
(From Efuru)	
Obi dịm ụtọ na o mere n'ihu m.	I was happy it happened in my face (p. 13).
Ya bụ na nke a bụ anya gị?	So this is your eyes [sic]? (p. 27) (changing the singular demonstrative pronoun and its verb into plural will ruin the folk idiom).
Ọrịa ọcha.	white disease (i.e. leprosy) (pp. 55 & 56).
ụkwara nta.	Small cough (i.e. tuberculosis).
Ị nụla olu di gị?	Have you heard the voice of your husband? (p. 95).
Ịmụ akwụkwọ	To learn book (p. 205).
Anyị amaghị akwụkwọ.	We do not know book (p. 206).
(From Idu)	
Ime na-apụ ya	Pregnancy is leaving her (p. 18).
Obi sie gị ike.	Let your heart be strong (p. 72).

O nwere ihe na-eme gị n'anya?	Is anything wrong with your eyes? (p. 179). (A non-Igbo speaker would think that the egg-seller is referring to Onyemuru's sight [physical eyes]. But the reference is to her head – her state of sanity i.e. 'Are you mad?').
Emela m ihu ọjọ n'ụtụtụ nkwọ a	Don't spoil my face this Nkwo morning (ie. Don't bring me bad luck . . .).

To still further intensify the folksiness of her folk characters, Nwapa imbues them with beliefs which are verifiable among the folk whose life-style she tries to capture. Reference has already been made to the 'Do's and Don'ts' of a pregnant woman. Others include, to cite only a few from the two novels:

(1) The belief that something unpleasant will happen to one's children if they are counted. In any case, 'children are not goats or sheep or yams to be counted' (Ef. 34).

(2) The belief that animals and not women should give birth to more than one baby at a time. The opposite is an abomination. A *dibia*, there-fore, wishes that 'Efuru [should] have one baby, one baby until the house is full' (Ef. 37).

(3) Confession by a woman that a child born of an extramarital affair does not belong to the legal husband is believed to be 'an abomination' (Ef. 64).

(4) The belief that not washing one's hands well after washing a dead body will make one 'forget things easily' (Ef. 93).

(5) The belief that sweeping a house at night is 'sweeping out the wealth in [the] house' (Ef. 269).

(6) The belief that every man's fate is written on the palms of his hands. 'When a misfortune is written there, no matter how good you are misfortune will always follow you' (Id. 24, see also p. 195).

(7) A strong belief in heredity, a concept which is akin to the Old Testament idea of 'the children's teeth' being 'set on edge' because their 'fathers [had] eaten sour grapes'[6] (Id. 114-15).

(8) Belief in totems. Thus Onyemuru almost gets a woman lynched because she 'imprisons' a tortoise, 'the owner of our clan in [a] basket' (Id. 180-2).

(9) The belief that if children do not eat before going to sleep, witches will 'give them food in their dreams' (Id. 184), and

(10) Finally, the concept that the woman is basically inferior to the man, a concept which underlies the folk attitude to, and treatment of, women.[7] Efuru's father, for example, inherits all his wives, except Efuru's mother from his late father (Ef. 22). Idu is automatically inherited by her husband's brother, Ishiodu (Id. 216–17). In other words, a wife is inherited from a father by a son, and from a brother by (usually) a younger brother. Her place is in her husband's bedroom and kitchen (Id. 41). More or less her husband's slave, she must not fight with her spouse, no matter what the provocation (Id. 70). It is shocking to her to hear that a wife eats the food cooked by her 'lord and master' (her husband) even when she is heavy with his baby (Id. 70–71). All intuition and no logic, the woman is intellectually inferior to the man. 'Usually intuition did their [women's] reasoning for them' (Ef. 208).

But Nwapa's attempt to root her characters in the Igbo folk soil does not end with these and other folk beliefs not mentioned in this paper. She uses folk narrators to tell the stories of Efuru and Idu. The result is, apart from the oral quality of the narratives, that there is a built-in folk superstition which permeates the plots and the characters. Because they are themselves deeply superstitious they blandly hand on to the reader their acceptance of mysterious and most incredible acts and ideas, as in the account of Efuru and her father's visit to a *dibia*. Immediately Efuru and her father 'entered the compound, the *dibia* [who is "almost blind"] shouted, "Nwashike Ogene, I am happy you are coming today with your daughter. But I won't see you today because your daughter is menstruating. My medicines will be ineffective if she comes nearer. When she finishes bring her to me." Efuru was [of course] spellbound' (Ef. 24). A less superstitious narrator, who is sceptical of the mythical omniscience of *dibias*, would have subtly (i.e. without seeming to be doing so), depending on her sophistication as a raconteur, provided the reader with an insight into the prescience of the near blind *dibia's* knowledge. Witness also Nwosu's dream about the death of Efuru's father. Nwosu has hardly pronounced the last word of his account when the truth of the dream is confirmed by the 'Boom! Boom! Boom!' of the cannon (Ef. 251).

In *Idu* the reader is almost taken in by Anamadi's magic way of getting food ready with incredible speed:

> Anamadi made the fire quickly, sliced the yam and put it over the fire. Then she cut ugu in bits, pounded the pepper and washed the dried fish. Soon the yam was ready. It was ready quickly and this was because she put a small slice of the yam on top of the cover of the pot. It is believed that when you are in a hurry and you do this, your yam will cook quickly (Id. 217).

The narrator has no doubt in her mind that the magic works. As a matter of fact, the folk narrator is so rooted in folk superstition that she implicitly believes, and by extension wants the reader to believe, that the liquidation of such beliefs as that which portrays twins as an abomination, is the cause of such modern day misfortunes (she calls them 'evils') as death from dog bite. Our ancestors, she insists through Uzoechi, would not believe it if someone went 'to the land of the dead' and told them 'that our people die of dog bite'. Nwasobi's affirmation is almost authorial.

> How can they believe it? ... They were pure. They kept all the laws of the land, so they lived a different life from the life we are living now (Id. 199).

The conscious defiance of folk values is indeed the cause of the tragedy of Efuru. Right from the dawn of her life, Efuru recognises the folk norms, but deliberately goes against them, thanks to her alliance with Uhamiri, the paradoxical feminist goddess of the lake. The conflict between the resilience of the folk values and Efuru's consciously inconsiderate attitude towards them is the cause of the unhappiness which engulfs her throughout the novel.

This is also true, to some extent, of Idu. Certainly the novel which bears her name is not as feminist oriented as *Efuru*. Uhamiri does not lay any open claim on her loyalty. The novel surely has a duplicate of Ajanupu in Nwasobi even if Nwasobi, is only a faint copy of that epitome of the Igbo folk culture or ways, including medicine, humour, beliefs, etc. But *Idu* lacks the feminist *coup de pilon* on an oppressive pig's head (Ef. 276) and other such guffaws at the expense of a pigheaded 'lord and master' (Ef. 224). Even Idu's ambition to bear a baby-girl first does not stem from any feminist ideology. She only wants a helper in her drudgery as a woman, wife and mother. 'A girl was very useful to her mother. She would help with the house when her mother went to the market. She would look after her subsequent sisters and brothers. It was an asset to have a girl first' (Id. 79). Yet by her death she deals an effective blow to the sexist folk expectation that a widowed wife must perforce marry her late husband's brother.

The folk are, indeed, under siege in *Efuru* and *Idu*; but they are not liquidated. In the Ajanupus and Nwasobis they have store-rooms that approximate to the mud wardrobes ('the room in room, very dark both in the daytime and at night ... used for storing valuable things') (Ef. 86) which they erect in their houses to secure their riches from fire, robbers and other emergencies.

Flora Nwapa's first two novels may not be masterpieces but they are deeply rooted in the soil of Igbo folklore.

NOTES

1. Flora Nwapa, *Efuru* (London: Heinemann, 1966), (hereafter cited as Ef.).
2. Flora Nwapa, *Idu* (London: Heinemann, 1970), (hereafter cited as Id.).
3. For an insight into the place of Mammy Water in the life of a community in whose river or lake she is believed to live, see Francis A. Arinze, *Sacrifice in Igbo Religion* (Ibadan: Ibadan University Press, 1970): 14–15.
4. Such a girl often becomes the wife of the lender – even if the lender is a woman.
5. Chinua Achebe, *Arrow of God* (1965; reprint, London: Heinemann, 1974): 21.
6. Ezekiel 18: 2 (King James's Version of *The Holy Bible*).
7. For a more detailed discussion on Flora Nwapa's portrayal of women in Igboland see Chidi Ikonné, 'The Society and Women's Quest for Selfhood in Flora Nwapa's Early Novels', *Kunapipi*, 6, 1 (1984): 68–78.

Oral Literature & Modern Nigerian Drama: The Example of Femi Osofisan

Muyiwa P. Awodiya

Femi Osofisan is the most talented and productive of the second generation of Nigerian dramatists. Though his works are yet to be well known outside Nigeria, he is fast building up the reputation of being the leading Nigerian dramatist after Wole Soyinka.[1] A radical writer and critic with an articulated commitment to a materialist, socialist and class perspective, Osofisan combines a radical ideology with a recognition of the importance of cultural traditions. He has consistently advocated and defended art that is anti-elitist, popular and accessible.[2] Like most leading Nigerian dramatists, Osofisan's dramaturgy often draws inspiration from traditional culture but he is distinguished by the fact that he uses the devices of oral literature for far more radical purposes than any other Nigerian playwright.

Certainly the most dominant trend in contemporary African literature is that of writers going back to their traditional roots to see what can be borrowed from oral literature to enrich written literature. Osofisan is of special interest in this respect because he has consistently employed the devices of oral literature in his drama. The effective manner in which these devices are used in his plays demands attention. Apart from their aesthetic functions, folklore techniques in Osofisan's plays often become the vehicle of critical thematic commentary on the state of the society.

This paper will attempt to show how Osofisan's works continue cultural traditions while advocating social change by employing the traditional motifs of oral history and beliefs, myth and narrative, magic and incantation, mystery, ritual and sacrifice, festival, proverb, and music and song, in his six full-length plays.[3]

Revolutionary Reconstruction of History, Myth and Legend

Osofisan uses elements of oral history, myth and legend in *The Chattering and the Song* and *Morountodun* in a subversive manner by exploiting the considerable power which tradition exerts in an effort to positively influence contemporary Nigerian life. In these plays, he radically revises and

105

reshapes familiar history, myth and legend in the light of contemporary realities in order to stress their dialectical dynamism, and to seek out fresher meanings from them. Furthermore, he exposes the ills of the society and provides the audience with his vision of a new social order.

The core of *The Chattering and the Song* is the play-within-a-play which is a re-enactment of an historical confrontation in 1885 between Latoye, the leader of a revolutionary Farmers Movement, and Alafin Abiodun, the king. For his own radical purposes, Osofisan reconstructs the recorded history of the nineteenth-century Yorubaland in the play-within-a-play to make Alafin Abiodun no longer the legendary hero who according to historians restored peace to his troubled kingdom.[4] On the contrary, Abiodun is depicted in the play as a tyrant who uses the claims of custom and divine sanction to exploit his subjects.

In line with the logic of the reconstructed history, Latoye, a member of the elite, is depicted as committing class suicide by abandoning his class and allying himself with the lower classes in their struggle against the oppression and brutality of King Abiodun. Thus Latoye contends that members of the ruling class have perverted the gods to secure themselves in power and enhance their selfish exploitation of the people:

> For centuries you have shielded yourselves with the gods. Slowly, you painted them in your colour, dressed them in your own cloak of terror, injustice and bloodlust. In your reign Abiodun, the elephant eats, and nothing remains for the antelope! The buffalo drinks and there is drought in the land![5]

If *The Chattering and the Song* typifies Osofisan's radical reconstruction of oral history to justify a revolutionary challenge to feudal power, *Morountodun* exemplifies his attempt to restate popular myths for the same revolutionary ends. In *Morountodun*, he reconstructs the Moremi myth and legend of the past to suit his revolutionary view on the political forces of oppression, injustice and corruption in contemporary Nigeria.

Legend relates that when the existence of ancient Ife was threatened by the frequent military onslaught of its Igbo neighbours, Queen Moremi abandoned her wealth and palatial splendour, infiltrated the enemy camp, studied their tricks and came back home to ensure victory for her army. In *Morountodun*, Osofisan yokes this legend with the 1969 popular farmers uprising in the old Western Nigeria. In that year, the Yoruba peasant farmers revolted against the oppression and excessive taxation by the government of that region. The peasants named their revolt *Agbekoya* (Yoruba word for 'Farmers Reject Exploitation').

In the play, the aristocratic Titubi, considering himself the present-day Moremi and egged on by the government agent Salami, infiltrates the peasants' ranks as a spy. But after being exposed to the peasant's way of life and experiencing their suffering, she, in a twist of fate, renounces her bourgeois heritage and becomes ideologically transformed to the farmers' cause:

Titubi: I went, and I returned, triumphant.
          But I am not the same as I went away.
          A lot has happened.[6]

The ancient Moremi myth has thus been re-fashioned in the typical strategy of subversion which is a fundamental characteristic of radicalising the familiar in Osofisan's dramaturgy. In the Moremi myth, Moremi served the ruling class. But in the re-fashioned myth, Osofisan makes the modern-day Moremi (Titubi) serve the ruled. Titubi denounces her legendary model Moremi, because she served the ruling class:

> I am not Moremi! Moremi served the state, was the state, was the spirit of the ruling class. But it is not true that the state is always right . . . Let a new life begin.[7]

Elements of Oral Narratives

While the thematic interest of *The Chattering and the Song* and *Morountodun* derives from a revolutionary re-interpretation of history, myth and legend, a number of Osofisan's plays attract our attention through their exploitation of the technical resources of folklore narrative. Oral narrative devices constitute the vehicle of plot and dramatic action in *Once Upon Four Robbers*, *Farewell to a Cannibal Rage* and *Morountodun*.

In these plays, Osofisan uses the traditional folk-tale approach of organising moonlight stories and riddles around a story-teller or narrator. The story-teller usually places himself at the edge of an audience in circular formation and shouts out the traditional introductory formula, '*Alo o*' (meaning I have a riddle). And the audience responds '*Aalo!*' (meaning we are listening). This way the story-teller captures the attention of, and establishes a rapport with, the audience. This also generates full audience participation in the theatre.

Once Upon Four Robbers opens in a traditional African moonlit atmosphere. The story-teller, by the use of the properties of indigenous dance, music and song, narrates his story through a dialectical process. The robbers who are paradoxically presented as the victims of a capitalist society, want to be saved from this society which is controlled by 'these modern men, money-hunting, evil-doing to amass property . . .'[8] The story-teller later reverses perspective and presents the robbers to the audience as 'Dangerous highwaymen, Despatchers of lives to heaven.'[9]

While using the familiar oral narrative technique, Osofisan nonetheless subverts the form in a number of ways purposely to remove the play from the realm of folktale[10] and elevate it to the level of incisive social criticism. He enlarges the scope of the folktale to project his ideological viewpoint which is that armed robbery and other social ills like hunger, unemployment, corruption and injustice are the products of a capitalist society. He asserts that the robbers are produced by the way the society is organised or disorganised and that there is a need to effect a decisive change in the structure of the (Nigerian) society.[11]

In order to build audience sympathy for the position in which the victims are represented as 'helpless' products of an unjust society, Osofisan allows the so-called victims (the robbers) to remain alive for the entire duration of the play. He employs the folktale device in an unconventional way to confront the contemporary phenomenon of armed robbery in Nigeria in a manner that shocks the audience into social awareness. For example, within the framework of the oral narrative adopted for the play, at the point of execution, a dialogue ensues between the robbers tied to the stakes and their executioners:

> Major: ... Serg, today the law is on the side of those who have, and in abundance, who are fed and bulging, who can afford several concubines. But tomorrow, that law will change. The poor will seize it and twist its neck. The starving will smash the gates of the supermarkets, the homeless will no longer yield in fear to your bulldozers. And your children, yes, your dainty, little children will be here where I stand now, on the firing block ...
> Sergeant: Enough! You'll not repent, I see. Company, take position!

Also the use of familiar performance modes like multiple role-playing and story-telling further generates full audience participation in the theatre. All the songs of Aafa, the story-teller, for instance, comment upon the actions as well as provide the story-line of the play.

Exploitation of Traditional Yoruba Belief in Divinities and Mysteries

The traditional Yoruba community has a complex cosmology and system of beliefs which Osofisan explores for creative inspiration for his entirely modern and revolutionary dramatic art. For instance, he exploits the Yoruba belief in divinities to portray Esu as an intermediary god in *Esu and the Vagabond Minstrels*. He also portrays Orunmila as a god of wisdom and guidance in *Farewell to a Cannibal Rage*.

Esu and the Vagabond Minstrels is about five vagabond musicians who have become jobless due to government proscription of entertainers. They trek from place to place, searching in vain for work, till they arrive at a crossroads where they meet Esu, the god of good as well as evil,[13] the mediator between man and the rest of the gods. Esu tests the vagabond musicians by giving them the magic power to cure suffering people. All but one of the musicians abuse the power by exploiting their patients and thus enriching themselves. Esu punishes the four greedy musicians and rewards only the musician who was compassionate and healed without amassing material wealth from his patients.

The belief of the Yoruba in Esu as the god of mediation and benevolence, who can provide children for the barren or riches for the poor, is also portrayed in the play. For example, the people who are in distress in the play offer sacrifices to placate Esu:

Omele: . . . People bring a lot of food and leave them on this crossroads.
Sin Sin: Why? What for?
Omele: As offering to Esu. From those searching for children, or for riches, or for a long life . . . So Esu is regarded as a kind of intermediary, between men and their wishes, between destiny and fulfilment.[14]

The use of the Esu motif in the play thus conforms entirely with the traditional folklore usage as instrument of moral instruction and the amelioration of human suffering.

The same faithfulness to tradition is also applicable in the interpretation of the role of the deity, Orunmila, in *Farewell to a Cannibal Rage*. In the play, the belief in Orunmila as the god of wisdom and guidance who must be consulted by the people when they want to take important decisions affecting their lives is demonstrated. Olabisi's mother, Titi, consults the *Babalawo*,[15] the priest of Orunmila, to seek his advice and guidance about the intended marriage of her daughter to Akanbi. This recourse to Orunmila is of vital importance since the two lovers are descendants of families in a bloody vengeance feud. Indeed, Olabisi's father had murdered Akanbi's father while Akanbi's uncle had murdered Olabisi's father in retaliation. Only Orunmila can show the true line of action in such a deal.

Furthermore, many of Osofisan's plays are informed by the use of the belief in the efficacy of mysterious powers such as incantations and magic. Plays like *Morountodun*, *Once Upon Four Robbers*, *Esu and the Vagabond Minstrels* and *The Chattering and the Song* employ incantations which involve the chanting of words purporting to have magical or mysterious powers. In *Morountodun*, for example, the character Marshall, uses the power of incantation to secure the support and approval of the dead and the living, and of trees and animals, in re-naming Titubi as Morountodun, to make the new name be propitious throughout her life:

Marshall: Now I call on this earth I am standing on. (Takes gourd from kokondi and pours libation. He softly chants an incantation . . .) I call on you trees and animals which people our forests and are our kinsmen. I summon the seeing eyes of our ancestors and you my dear friends standing . . . I name her Morountodun![16]

The belief in magic as a means of bending or tapping elemental or supernatural forces for man's use constitutes the vehicle of dramatic actions in these plays.

The Aafa in *Once Upon Four Robbers*, for example, gives the robbers magic power to rob their victims by enchanting them with their songs and dancing for their victims:

Aafa: ... Once you begin to sing, anyone within hearing distance stops whatever he is doing and joins. He will sing and dance and then head for his home to sleep. And he won't wake till the next morning.[17]

Ritual and Sacrifice

Rituals and ceremonies like child-naming, marriage, installation of chiefs or kings, initiation, and burial rites are daily occurrences among the Yorubas. Sacrifices are also offered by them to the gods for various purposes – propitiating the gods in order to avert calamity; atoning for offences committed; expressing gratitude to the divinities for their blessings and guidance. Osofisan uses elements of both ritual and sacrifice in his plays.

In *No More the Wasted Breed*, Elusu, the goddess of inland waters, is angry with human beings for polluting her waters. She therefore overflows her banks, causing floods, food scarcity, and a plague that afflicts children, including Biokun's son, Erindo. Olokun, the sea god of justice rebukes Elusu for her excesses and upholds Biokun's protest against the old custom of using human beings as carriers and sacrifice to the gods. Biokun offers sacrifice to Olokun in order to save the life of his child. The stage direction gives a graphic description.

(Beachside, sea in flood. Biokun comes in over narrow muddy path, carrying a pot, earthen, chalked white. His own face is partially chalked white too, his body naked, save for a white wrapper round his waist. He walks in slowly, solemn, seeming to count his steps. Then puts the pot down. He kneels besides it, facing the sea, making strange gestures.)

Biokun: Olokun, here's the offering, warm in my hand. Here I am. Let the boy live! (He begins to intone the chant to Olokun.)[18]

Dramatic Appropriation of the Festival Motif

Festivals in African communities are occasions of merriment and joyous celebration through which ritual propitiation and sacrifice are offered by the community in order to control and dominate the natural forces around them.[19] Osofisan uses festival motifs to realise the theme of some of his plays. For example, *Morountodun* and *Esu* are set in a typical indigenous festival atmosphere to celebrate harvest. *Esu and the Vagabond Minstrels* opens with a festive celebration as the stage directions indicate:

(Lights come up on a festive scene. A community in obvious celebration ... at the close of harvest ... Community leaders sit on a slightly raised platform, while the rest are on mats, stools, etc. Each holds a calabash cup, while younger men and women, bearing large gourds, go round serving (palmwine) ...)[20]

The calendrical celebration of harvest is an event of social, religious and economic importance in the life of the African community. In these plays, most of the action takes place in the forest (*Morountodun*) and at a crossroads (*Esu*) – typical festival settings. The series of movements and celebrations in the forest and at the crossroads that take us through the action of the play are akin to the various rites performed by the community in a festival context. The various dances and movements symbolise aspects of a festival celebration. The peasants, for example, sing and dance the song of harvest celebration in praise of Moremi in *Morountodun* when Titubi is being initiated into their community. As usual this is made explicit in the stage directions (p. 40).

Linguistic Localisation through Proverb, Parable and Riddle

The devices of proverb, parable and riddle are borrowed by Osofisan from oral literature to localise his plays in Yoruba culture. Apart from serving as a means of cultural preservation, these devices also facilitate access to the plays through the use of familiar images and sayings. This enables Osofisan not only to communicate with the audience who share the same cultural values with him but also to enrich their aesthetic experience through striking symbolic structures.

During the confrontation between Latoye and Abiodun in *The Chattering and the Song*, for example, Latoye asserts with a memorable proverb that he is more powerful than Abiodun: 'The sapling which tries to halt the passage of the elephant will be plucked from its roots!'[21]

Similarly the danger of indiscriminate love is conveyed in *Farewell to a Cannibal Rage* through an appropriate parable:

Baba Soye: I shall tell you a story, Bisi.
Olabisi: A story?
Baba Soye: A fable. Like those told to children in moonlight.[22]

Also the peasant women at the streamside convey fun and amusement when they tease Titubi with a love riddle in reference to her relationship with Marshall in *Morountodun*:

Mama Kayode: ... A riddle! Shall I tell it?
Women: Tell it!
Mama Kayode: Listen. The he-goat wears a beard, the she-goat also wears a beard: Oba Lailo! ...
Wura: Titubi, do you care to enlighten us?
Titubi: Why me? This is a trap isn't it? I withdraw from the game ...
Wura: All right, I'll solve the riddle. Love! Someone's in love ...[23]

Evocative Dramatic Embellishment through Music, Song and Dance

There are hardly any of Osofisan's plays that do not employ the traditional Yoruba music, song and dance. They possess participatory qualities because they evoke responses from the audience. They serve as means through which the audience actually partake of the action on the stage. The playwright manipulates these elements not only to convey a sensually rich atmosphere but also to provide the Brechtian link between the action of the plot and the thematic horizon of the play. For example the 'Song of Khaki and Agbada' in *Esu and the Vagabond Minstrels* indicts both the military and civilian governments of corruption in Nigeria:

> Khaki and Agbada
> De two dey waka together
> 'with immediate effect'
> He don chop de treasury
> 'With immediate despatch!'
> He buy jet for Mecca
> Fly to Rome for shopping . . .[24]

Conclusion

Given his ideological orientation, it is not surprising that Osofisan consciously employs the devices of oral literature and the traditional performance mode in his plays. His conscious intention is to create a popular theatre form with which the masses easily identify. Through this form, he is able to elicit responses from his audience and mobilise them to participate in the drama, thus breaking the 'fourth-wall' and bringing drama outside the stage to the level of the popular audience.

Osofisan also uses oral literature as a source of ideological attack that challenges and criticises contemporary Nigeria in which the social, political and economic arrangements benefit only the ruling class. The desire for a new social order in which the masses shall be free from the existing oppression of the hegemony is implicit in his theatre.

Oral literary forms are used to reinforce or criticise and transform existing values as well as to communicate, through familiar routes, with the audience. The aesthetic success which has accompanied Osofisan's and other writers' appropriation of oral literary forms so as to lift written literature to a new height may have an implied lesson for the political leaders of Africa. It may well be that Africans must go back to their traditional roots to seek the basis for economic, political and scientific innovation and progress if they are to succeed in building a modern society.

But whatever the larger implications, Osofisan's use of the elements of oral literature not only brings his plays closer to the ritual origin of drama, but even more importantly enhances their aesthetic appeal to the audience.

NOTES

1. His play, *Morountodun*, won the Association of Nigerian Author's (ANA) Best Drama Prize in 1983; and his poetry, *The Minted Coins*, won the ANA's Best Poetry Prize in 1987. He has also written a well acclaimed novel, *Kolera Kolej*, and his serialised short stories often make *The Guardian* on Sunday a prized newspaper in Nigeria.
2. Personal interview with Femi Osofisan on 19 July, 1986.
3. *The Chattering and the Song* (Ibadan: Ibadan University Press, 1977); *Morountodun and Other Plays* (Ikeja: Longman Nigeria Limited, 1982). (The volume contains two other plays apart from *Morountodun: No More the Wasted Breed* and *Red is the Freedom Road*); *Once Upon Four Robbers* (Ibadan: BIO Educational Service Ltd., 1980); *Farewell to a Cannibal Rage* (Ibadan: Evans Brothers Nigeria Ltd., 1986); *Esu and the Vagabond Minstrels* (Ibadan: New Horn Press, publication forthcoming). He is also the author of the following plays: *A Restless Run of Locusts* (Ibadan: Onibonoje Publishers, 1975); *Who's Afraid of Solarin?* (Ibadan: Scholars Press Nigeria Ltd., 1978); *Midnight Hotel* (Ibadan: Evans Brothers Nigeria Ltd., 1986); Two One-Act Plays that contain *The Oriki of a Grasshopper* and *Altine's Wrath* (Ibadan: New Horn Press, 1986). All subsequent references to these plays are from these editions.
4. Samuel Johnson, *The History of the Yorubas* (Lagos: C.S.C. Bookshops, 1921): 186. See other histories as J.F. Ade Ajayi and Robert Smith, *Yoruba Warfare in the Nineteenth Century* (London: Cambridge University Press and Institute of African Studies, University of Ibadan, 1971); J.A. Atanda, *An Introduction to Yoruba History* (Ibadan: Ibadan University Press, 1960); Michael Crowder, *The Story of Nigeria* (London: Faber, 1962); and Robert Smith, *Kingdoms of the Yoruba* (London: Methuen, 1969).
5. Osofisan, *The Chattering and the Song*: 45.
6. Osofisan, *Morountodun*: 60.
7. Osofisan: 70.
8. Osofisan, *Once Upon Four Robbers*: viii.
9. Osofisan: viii.
10. A folktale in Yoruba custom teaches a simple moral lesson only. See Richard M. Dorson, ed., *African Folklore* (New York: Doubleday and Company, Inc., 1972).
11. Femi Osofisan in an interview with *The African Guardian* January 8, 1987: 31.
12. Osofisan, *Once Upon Four Robbers*: 63.
13. Esu in pedestrian terms is the trickster god who upsets the balance of forces. But he is given more functions by Olodumare as the mediator between man and the rest of the gods; and between man and the Supreme Being, Olodumare. For more information see such books as J. Omosade Awolalu, *Yoruba Beliefs and Sacrificial Rites* (London: Longman Group Ltd., 1979); G.J. Afolabi Ojo, *Yoruba Culture* (London: University of Ife and University of London Press Ltd., 1966).
14. Osofisan, *Esu and the Vagabond Minstrels*: 10.
15. Orunmila is the Yoruba god of wisdom or divination. He is also referred to as the oracle who is consulted for advice and guidance. The method by which

Orunmila, the oracle, is consulted is called Ifa and the priest of Ifa is the *Babalawo* who interprets the wishes of Orunmila to the people and recommends the appropriate sacrifice.

16. Osofisan, *Morountodun*: 74.
17. Osofisan, *Once Upon Four Robbers*: 22.
18. *No More the Wasted Breed*: 91. Also see *Esu and the Vagabond Minstrels*: 22; *Red is the Freedom Road*: 124; and *Morountodun*: 34.
19. See Oyin Ogunba's 'Traditional African Festival Drama', *Theatre in Africa*, Oyin Ogunba and Abiola Irele, eds., (Ibadan: Ibadan University Press, 1978); and S.O. Biobaku, ed., *Sources of Yoruba History* (London: Oxford University Press, 1973).
20. Osofisan, *Esu and the Vagabond Minstrels*: 1.
21. Osofisan, *The Chattering and the Song*: 41.
22. Osofisan, *Farewell To a Cannibal Rage*: 43.
23. Osofisan, *Morountodun*: 68.
24. Osofisan, *Esu and the Vagabond Minstrels*: 2.

French-Language African Drama & the Oral Tradition: Trends & Issues

John Conteh-Morgan

Introduction

The oral tradition – in the sense of a stock of oral narratives and their performance traditions on the one hand, and of a body of beliefs, customs and practices on the other – constitutes the single most important source of inspiration for the African dramatist writing in French. Even when he seems farthest from its concerns, like when he is making an artistic statement on issues of contemporary relevance, or of general human significance, he still remains firmly tethered to it, borrowing from its resources of legend, heroic song, myth and folktale not only characters (human, animal and mythical) but also subjects, situations and formal procedures.

In this article, I shall attempt in broad outline a survey of the multiple levels and the specific nature of the relationship between this drama and the oral tradition both in the latter's ancient and modern manifestations.[1] Is it a dynamic and creative relationship in which new linkages and meanings are constructed from old texts and beliefs, or is it one governed by rules of strict fidelity to the inspirational source? I will be making references to a variety of plays, but with the exception of Eugène Dervain's *La reine scélérate* (1968) in the first part of the article, and Zinsou's *On joue la comédie* (1972) in the second, both of which are discussed at length, the rest are mentioned only in illustration of certain aspects of the subjects under consideration.

The Thematic Legacy

A notable feature of the oral tradition that is extensively exhibited by francophone drama is a preoccupation with history, especially heroic history. In spite of their orality, the traditional societies of Tropical Africa, as is now widely recognised, do not lie 'beyond the days of self-conscious history ... enveloped in the dark mantle of the night.'[2] They display a high degree of historical consciousness that is deeply embedded in their oral traditions and that constitutes a vital aspect of their outlook.[3]

115

In addition to recording a past that sometimes stretches back centuries, these traditions – especially in the highly-centralised former kingdoms (Mali, Benin, Dahomey, Segu Tukulor and so on) in the region now occupied by francophone African states – provide, by their historical chronicles of how power came to be acquired, what Ruth Finnegan has described as ' "a mythical charter" . . . for the existing distribution of political power.'[4]

Such is their importance that their custody and dissemination are entrusted to professionals popularly known in French-speaking Africa as 'griots'. One of them, made famous by Djibril Tamsir Niane in his *Soundjata ou l'épopée mandingue* (1960) explains their task thus:

> We griots know the history of kings and their kingdoms; this is why we make the best royal advisers. Every great king needs a griot to perpetuate his memory, for it is our duty to preserve the memory of kings. (*Soundjata*, p. 78)[5] There would be no heroes if their actions were consigned to oblivion; we act to elicit the admiration of the living and secure the respect of the yet unborn (*Soundjata*, p. 108).

It is this role of chronicler and celebrator of the past, described here by Kouyaté, that constitutes one of the enduring legacies of the oral tradition to modern African drama in French.

Most francophone African plays are devoted to the presentation of events and figures from Africa's recent or distant past.[6] Many of these, like Jean Pliya's *Kondo le requin* (1981), Cheikh Ndao's *L'exil d'Albouri* (1967) or Sory Konaké's *Le grand destin de Soundjata* (1973) are set in clearly identifiable time-schemes and deal with acknowledged historical figures. Others, however, like Charles Nokan's *Abraha Pokou, une grande africaine* (1970), Eugène Dervain's play of the same name (both about Queen Pokou, the alleged founder of the Baoulé people of the Ivory Coast), and Ola Balogun's *Shango* (1968), also on a presumed one-time ruler of the Yoruba empire of Oyo, are set outside of historical time. They recount the careers of heroes or heroines whose factual existence, assuming they ever existed, has been obscured by time and the myth-making imagination.

But whatever the degree of their historicity, these plays like the chronicles of the 'griot', have one thing in common – a celebratory nature. They are like canticles intoned to the memory of illustrious ancestors: Gbéhanzin, the nineteenth-century ruler of ancient Dahomey, self-styled the 'shark' in affirmation of his will to protect his country from foreign invasion in the Pliya play; Albouri, also the nineteenth-century ruler of the Wolof kingdom in present-day Senegal in the Ndao play, and Sunjata the thirteenth-century founder of the Mandingo empire in the Sory Konaké work. Other warrior-kings or heroine-queens whose names have provided titles to several plays or whose deeds have been sung in drama include Lat Dior (1842–1886) the 'damel' or king of Cayor and Baol, in present-day Senegal, who chose suicide rather than submit to the French troops of Faideherbe; El-Hadj Omar (1797–1864) an intrepid fighter against the

French and founder of the Tukulor empire which, at its height, extended over a thousand kilometres; Shaka (1787-1828) empire-builder and king of the Zulus; Yangouman the queen of Abron in Atta Koffi's *Le trône d'or* (1969) and Ba Mousso Sano, King Tiéba's wife in Massa Makan Diabaté's *Une si belle leçon de patience* (1972).

In lush rhetorical language, their patriotism, real but often purely imagined, is extolled. Through a dramatic re-creation of their heroic struggles to defend or expand their territories, and of the elaborate court splendour and ceremonial that attended their lives, is conveyed a living sense of pre-colonial African societies at their most glorious and, in their defeat, a sense of lost heritage.

It is interesting to note in this regard that the playwrights most interested in heroic history – the Senegalese Ndao, Ibrahima Sall, Abdou Anta Ka, Thierno Ba, Amadou Cissé Dia; the Guinean Djibril Niane, Condetto Nénékhaly-Camara; the Malian Seydou Badian, Sory Konaké, Massa Makan Diabaté; André Salifou of Niger and Jean Pliya of Benin to name but a few – are all descended from highly centralised former empires with strong 'griot' and, by extension, heroic historical traditions. By extolling in their plays the valour of various rulers, these dramatists are merely pursuing, in literate form, an ancestral practice. The emphases now as then are on the same things: military exploits, heroic deeds, noble ancestry.

The Formal Legacy

But the cultural continuity between the oral tradition and francophone drama goes beyond content – a preoccupation with heroic history – to form itself. French-language African plays have appropriated some of the formal features, conventions and procedures of oral historiography as these are embodied in the oral narrative most concerned with history: the legend.[7] One such feature characteristic of the historical legend is its tendency to move from the world of observable historical facts to which it is moored and of which it purports to be an account, into that of fantasy and magic; to crystallise all the action around a central figure, the hero, whose deeds are then magnified, embellished and swamped in an atmosphere of the supernatural, in order to confer mythical status on him.

Thus Sunjata in Niane's version of the legend is born to a mother who is half-buffalo and half-woman. He miraculously gains the power of his limbs after a seven-year period of congenital paralysis and uproots an enormous baobab tree in a show of supernatural strength. Douga, the king of Koré in the epic *Da Monzon de Segou*, can appear and disappear at will by merely biting at his talisman. When, in the battle against Da Monzon, he is told of his army's collapse, he seeks refuge underwater in the lair of his divinity the sacred cayman (crocodile).

This drift towards fantasy and myth inherent in the legend is clearly present in the African history play in French. When such a play starts, the hero, be he for example a Patrice Lumumba (in Aimé Césaire's *Une saison au Congo*[8], 1970), an Albouri or a Gbéhanzin, is usually an ordinary human being grappling with problems which, however intractable, are very human: the cultural, economic and political reconstruction of a disunited and hitherto colonised society in the case of Lumumba; the defence of sovereignty against the vastly superior might of the French in the case of Albouri and Gbéhanzin. By the time it ends, however, these very human and social forces in conflict have been endowed with non-human qualities – with the heroes invariably achieving near-mythical stature and embodying in defeat (they are usually defeated) that which is noblest in their societies.

Thus Lumumba becomes 'an invincible idea', 'pollen dust', 'a tree', while Albouri, the symbol of Djoloff independence, becomes 'a star broken free from the heavens', and his people, 'eternal spirit-wanderers galloping across oceans at full bridle and haunting the dreams of the brave' (*L'exil d'Albouri*, p. 90). The defeat of the hero in other words is transcended by a drive towards mythical immortality. His physical death is transmuted into moral triumph.

This epic quality of the francophone historical playwright's imagination – freely admitted to by Ndao who defines his dramatic purpose in *L'exil d'Albouri* as being 'to contribute to the creation of myths that galvanise the people ...' (p. 15) – is forcefully brought out by Oyie Ndzie when he observes:

> (Francophone) dramatic practice becomes ipso facto mythological that is 'a utopian reconstitution of the real'. The heroes and situations depicted are held up as sublime examples, ultimate references and olympian values. They crystallize all the quintessential qualities of perfection of the society to which they are held up.[9]

Another formal feature of the oral historical narrative in the francophone African play is the episodic nature of the action. The organisation of events in plays like *Kondo le requin*, *L'exil d'Albouri*, Seydou Badian's *La mort de Chaka* (1962) or especially Nokan's *Abraha Pokou*, takes its interest mainly from what it progressively reveals of the hero's character, rather than from a sequential plot arrangement depicting development and change. It is principally concerned with exhibiting in a series of representative episodes, idealised qualities of character in the heroes, which are supposed to exemplify certain permanent truths or move audiences to emulate them.

But to say that francophone history plays are mostly character rather than action-centred is not to say that they are lacking in theatrical appeal. Indeed they display a vivid quality of spectacle and theatre, also a feature of the oral historical narrative. This is conveyed by the recourse to colourful ceremonies: enthronements, funerals, the evocation of battle scenes and the visual and rhetorical display of heroic deeds.

Kondo le requin is a good example of this feature. Striking elements of spectacle in it include in Act 2, Scene 2, the highly ceremonial coronation ritual of Gbéhanzin; the procession in the hierarchical order of traditional notables: the *migan* (prime minister), the *mehou* (preceptor to the royal family and minister of external relations), the *adjaho* (minister of justice), pledging allegiance to their colourfully-attired new king; the display of symbolic items representing power and authority – the 'sacred amulette', the 'blue pearl necklace', the 'royal staff'; the formal praise-names by which the king is addressed, and the farewell ceremony before his surrender.

A feature of the oral tradition that persists in modern francophone drama is the use of the cultural figure of the 'griot'. Poet, dancer and narrator all rolled into one, he is also, by his ability to play the role of different characters, an actor.[10] In modern plays, he is mostly a kind of presenter of the play and a commentator on its action and hidden meanings, as is Djeli Madi in *Le grand destin de Soundjata*, Latsoukabé in Amadou Cissé's *Les derniers jours de Lat Dior* (1965), and Maliba in Ndao's *Le fils de l'Almamy* (1973). But in others like Eugène Dervain's *La reine scélérate* (1968) or *L'exil d'Albouri*, he is integrated as a character. In fact in the former play, he is a key actor, as it is his defection to the court of the king of Koré that sparks off the murderous conflict between the kingdoms of Segou and Koré.

The influence of the oral historical narrative also manifests itself in the francophone dramatist's use of colourful language, especially of the panegyric technique of formalised praises and addresses sung to the object of praise. Thus Kondo is addressed as the 'king of pearls' (p. 23), 'the rising sun' (p. 18), 'master of the dawn' (p. 24), while the sun-god is described by the griot in *L'exil d'Albouri*, Samba, as 'the breath of the buffalo in the savannah' (p. 21) and the king as:

> *Tison Ardent vomi par les flancs du lion*
> *en plein midi . . . l'éléphant, l'astre*
> *du zénith, le lion de Guilé* (p. 21).

> (Flaming Fire Brand thrown up from the
> lion's flanks at full noon . . . the
> elephant, the star at its zenith, the
> lion of Guilé).

Finally, the most obvious legacy of the oral tradition to francophone drama are the non-verbal elements of music, song and dance. There is hardly a play that does not have recourse to these elements. And their functions range from the creation of mood, local colour and spectacle, through being an interlude between events, to pure entertainment, as in the case of Oyono-Mbia's *Trois prétendants . . . un mari* (1964) where the stage directions specifically invite the audience in the last scene to join in the dancing and merriment. On occasion, however, music, song and dance are more than merely decorative. They are a supplement to dialogue and contribute to dramatic action. In Thierno Ba's very musical *Bilbassy* (1980) the *lagyah* tune reminds Samba, the son of the late King Guéladio, that he has now come of age and that he must fight for his father's throne against the usurper Konko. A crucial piece of dramatic action in other words, is precipitated by a tune.

From Epic to Drama – three examples of adaptations

But the generic relationship between the historical legend and modern francophone drama sometimes goes beyond the mere borrowing of theme or elements of form, to the dramatisation of actual historical or semi-historical *texts* of the oral tradition. The following are examples of such dramatised texts; Dervain's two plays *La reine scélérate* and *La langue et le scorpion* from the epic *Da Monzon de Ségou, épopée bambara* (1972), collected and published by Lilyan Kesteloot and Hampaté Ba; Sory Konaké's *Le grand destin de Soundjata* from the Sunjata epic, written versions of which include (in English) (Gordon Innes' *Sunjata* (1974) and Niane's *Soundjata* (already referred to), Charles Nokan's *Abraha Pokou, une grande africaine* from a Baoulé myth of which two written accounts exist: Bernard Dadié's in *Légendes et poèmes* (1966) and Maximilien Quénum's 'La légende des Baoulé' in *Légendes africaines: Côte d'Ivoire, Soudan, Dahomey* (1946).

But the relationship between these plays and the oral narrative texts which they adapt for the stage is far from being uniform. It ranges from the extreme licence of Nokan's work to the total subservience of Konaké's. In the Nokan play, the legend which narrates the exodus of the Baoulé people of present-day Ivory Coast from their prosperous lands to escape destruction from an enemy tribe, has been reinterpreted and secularised to convey a revolutionary twentieth-century political vision. Thus the exodus which in the tale is from invading neighbours, has become a 'Long March', and Queen Pokou, a female Mao-Tsetung (a quotation from the Chinese leader is incidentally put in epigraph to the play) leads her people from a feudal and oppressive system into a fiercely republican one that knows neither class nor sex differences.

But Nokan has not only given a radical pattern of meaning to his source-text, his 'hypotext', as some modern theorists of intertextuality call it,[11] he has also significantly changed its tone. Where the legend, especially Quénum's version of it, bathes in poetry and the supernatural, the play is rationalistic and prosaic in the extreme. An element that receives rationalistic treatment, for example, is the episode in the legend where Queen Pokou is able to secure safe passage across a river for herself and her people only after sacrificing her child, Agamemnon-like, to the river god. In the play, the sacrificial aspect has been left out. Instead of hippopotami (Dadié's account) or baobab trees (Quénum's) magically linking up tail to head or root to branch to form a bridge which then disappears once the fleeing party has crossed over, there are energetic men swimming across the river to summon the help of friendly tribesmen.

Nokan's impatience with what he sees as the irrationalities of myth, his advocacy for modern Africa of an outlook to nature and society that is informed by scientific rationalism and not magic is welcome and merits the most serious consideration.[12] But art and propaganda (even for an excellent cause such as Nokan's) have never been easy bedfellows and Nokan's attempt to marry them fails very badly. Not because his play is on the realistic mode, but because it does not develop credible dramatic situations, conflicts and characters. It is a tissue of slogans and lessons on civic responsibility.

Konaké on the other hand takes no liberties with his 'hypotext'. There is total similarity between the two: similarity in the events described and their sequence, from the prophecy to Naré Maghan, king of the Mandingo, that to him will be born a son who will be the eternal pride of the kingdom, to its fulfilment; similarity also in the characters depicted and the main theme, that of destiny. No attempt is made to demythify *à la Nokan* the mystery surrounding Sunjata's birth or the extraordinary powers of his Susu enemy Sumanguru Kanté. The only change that Konaké has brought to bear on the legend is in its presentation. Instead of the totally narrated piece of the original, we now have sequences told by a story-teller/performer, alternating with dramatic portions performed by the characters evoked. But as if to insist on its otherwise totally traditional form, Konaké has the 'griot' accompany his narrative on his guitar and remind the spectator that what he is going to take part in is '*une veillée*', an evening of traditional story-telling.

Between the extremes of these two plays stands the more substantial of Dervain's dramatisations of the Da Monzon epic, *La reine scélérate*. Here the playwright tries to be both faithful to the oral text and creative at the same time. He respects its main story-line: the war between Da Monzon, prince of Ségou and King Douga of Koré, ostensibly over the defection of the former's griot Tiécoura Danté; the defeat of the king of Koré, his subsequent suicide and the murder of his Queen, Saran, by the victorious forces.

But this is where the similarities end. For Dervain's aim is not to write a historical play, but to use the materials of a known, historical text to create drama and more specifically tragic drama. What attracts him in the epic is the tragic love theme – that of a young queen, Saran, whose all-consuming passion for a foreign prince, Da Monzon, leads her inexorably to betray her husband and fatherland.

In the end, however, all her dreams come to nought. Not only does her betrayed husband die, and his kingdom is completely destroyed, she too is killed before the hoped-for nuptials with her victorious lover, and her favourite court-poet Tiécoura Danté also commits suicide. Tiécoura, the man who in a sense sparked off the entire tragedy when, on an embassy to the court of King Douga of Koré before his defection, he captivated the young queen's mind with enchanting epic tales of the court of Ségou, its glamour and dashing eighteen-year old prince, Da Monzon:

> *Son élégance, est celle des seuls*
> *grands de ce monde: l'aigle, le cheval du Sahel . . .*
> *Sous sa peau vibre la plus fine musculature et son*
> *tient est d'ébène . . . Princess . . . (p. 30)*

('His elegance, Princess, [he assured her] is that of the great of
this world: an eagle, a horse of the Sahel . . .
beneath whose mahogany skin lies the finest
network of muscles imaginable.')

Saran, a Bovary-like character, fell in love with the romance of the tale and its prince even before meeting him. Long before Tiécoura decided to defect, she would declaim the tale's most poetic lines to console herself. And these were always about Da Monzon. So when Saran finally sees Da Monzon in her husband's court, the reader is not surprised that she literally loses control of herself. Events unfold from this point on with a tragic inevitability:

> *Aujourd'hui, personne au monde, aucune force,*
> *aucun fétiche ne sera capable de me retenir*
> *ici. Je viens de découvrir mon véritable destin.*
> *J'ai vu Da: je n'ai plus qu'un seul désir, une*
> *seule volonté, le suivre où il va, être avec*
> *lui à chaque instant de sa vie, le tenir dans*
> *mes bras et me soumettre à sa loi. J'ai vu Da.*
> *(p. 33).*

(From today, no one in the world, no force,
no magic will be able to keep me here. I've
just discovered my true destiny. I've seen Da:
I now have but one desire, one wish: to follow
him wherever he goes, to be with him every
minute of his life, to hold him in my arms
and to submit to his will. I've seen Da).

In the hands of Dervain then the Da Monzon epic has been transformed into a beautiful and powerful tragedy of love.

But to obtain this result the playwright has had to effect certain changes on the original material. Characters and situations have been more developed and the order of events changed somewhat. An example of such a change occurs in Act 3, Scene 16 and concerns the circumstances of Saran's death. In the epic, she is killed by Da Monzon's soldiers only after he refuses to be persuaded that having betrayed her husband, she cannot be trusted or be worthy of him. In the play, on the other hand, she is mistakenly killed by over-zealous Segovian soldiers who, on Da's orders,

she has heard about him, and sees him in the end only out of curiosity. But even when she discovers a fatal attraction for him, she shows some measure of self-restraint, agonising at one point over the prospect of having to betray her husband. 'Was it right,' she is reported as asking herself, 'to betray the man who had married her? – forcibly, no doubt, because she was his subject.' (p. 32).

No such moral dilemma plagues the Saran of the play. From the outset, she appears as the helpless victim of a destructive passion to which she will sacrifice anything:

> *Il m'importe peu d'être reine en ce pays. Il m'importe encore moins*
> *d'être couverte d'or et d'argent: je ne serai jamais heureuse,*
> *prisonnière que je suis en ce palais . . . où il n'y a pas de bonheur,*
> *il n'y a pas non plus de patrie!*
> (p. 40)

> I care little about being a queen in this land.
> I care even less about being draped in gold
> and silver: I'll never be happy, the prisoner
> that I am in this palace . . . And wherein there
> is no happiness, speak not of a fatherland

Where the Saran of the epic conveniently discovers marital problems only *after* seeing Da, Dervain's Saran experiences them well before, even before realising that the knight of the tales and of her dreams will ever come her way. In a sense, if she fed her imagination so copiously on tales of glamour and chivalry, it was a means of escape from the situation of a young lady forced into marriage with an ageing ruler. She complains:

> *Douga m'a choisie comme une noix de cola rose et il a dit: 'C'est*
> *celle-là que je veux!' Devrais-je avoir plus d'égards envers celui*
> *qui n'en a pas eu envers moi?*
> (p. 39).

> Douga singled me out as one would a pink
> colanut and said: 'That's the one I want!'
> Should I now show consideration to someone
> who has never shown any towards me?

By rooting Saran's romantic longings, adulterous love for Da and subsequent treachery in her unhappy marriage, Dervain is inviting attention to the traditional practice of forced marriages. The epic which purports to be a historical account of specific events in Bambara history has also now provided the framework for a statement on a contemporary social problem.

From Historical Narratives, Rituals and Customs to Drama

So far, we have seen that oral historical narratives provide the bulk of material used by the French-language African dramatist. It must be emphasised that other forms of oral narratives – notably the folktale – also provide material, although they are used to a much lesser degree. Examples of plays based on this genre are Birago Diop's *L'os de Mor Lam* (1977) and the more recent *La tortue qui chante* (1987) by the Togolese, Agbota Zinsou. More recently, ritual ceremonies (especially healing, initiation and purification rituals) have also provided the basis, both in terms of their content and structure, for a new type of francophone drama. This 'ritual-theatre', as it is called, 'is constructed', in the words of its leading theorist, 'from a synthesis of different rituals, the relevant elements of which have been extracted for use, while the others judged outdated have been rejected.'[13]

Although its practitioners (the Ivory Coast-based Camerounian researcher and playwright, Werewere Liking, and Marie-José Hourantier, the French ethnologist and ritual-theatre theoretician) insist on the aesthetic as opposed to religious dimensions of their enterprise, the function they assign to the new theatre which they are at pains to create is not different from the religious/therapeutic function of traditional ritual ceremonies. Just as purification/healing rituals, for example, aim to restore the equilibrium (psychic in the case of individuals, social in that of communities) broken by the eruption of disorder – incest, murder, disease and so on – so their plays seek to 'purge' (in Aristotle's sense of 'catharsis') the spectator of his fantasies, traumas and anxieties.

Plays like *La puissance de Um* (1979) and *Une nouvelle terre* (1980), written by Werewere Liking and produced by Hourantier, who significantly describes herself as 'The Master of Ceremonies' rather than 'The Producer', are really psychodramas. In the Ivory Coast where they have so far been produced, their success, as the critic Barthélémy Kotchy reports,[14] has been very limited. The idea that the theatregoer is a patient who needs to be 'cleansed' is clearly one that will have problems in a continent where the theatre is expected first and foremost to explore social and political problems and not psychological conundrums.

In addition to oral literary forms and rituals, the oral tradition's stock of beliefs and social customs also provide a rich source of inspiration, especially to the comic dramatist. Polygamy, the extended family, pre-arranged marriages, witchcraft and magic are among the many aspects that are given critical examination in plays like Oyono-Mbia's *Trois pretendants . . . un mari* and *La marmite de Koka Mbala* (1966) by the Congolese writer Guy Menga.

The Modern Oral Tradition and Drama

So far this article has used the term oral tradition to mean that tradition of literature whose origins stretch back to pre-colonial Africa and the beliefs associated with it. While this type of oral tradition continues to flourish, to attract scholarly attention and to enjoy funding and promotion from African Tourist Boards, it must be emphasised that it is by no means the only type currently in existence in Africa.

A modern, oral traditional form of literature and especially of theatre has fast been evolving too. Urban as opposed to rural, popular in preoccupation and comic in tone as opposed to dynastic and heroico-tragic, the preserve of no special caste but rather belonging to the general mass of the emerging working class, this new form combines elements of the ancient oral tradition (whose heroics it sometimes parodies) and of the popular culture of urban agglomerations. One such form of theatre in a francophone country is the 'concert-party' of Togo, and it is its relationship with a scripted play in French, *On joue la comédie* that will be considered next.

First published in 1975 this prize-winning play tells the story of the futile attempts by a group of black street actors to improvise a play on apartheid in the streets of Johannesburg. First interrupted by policemen who suspect them of being terrorists masquerading as actors, they are further prevented from staging their play by spectators who are either continuously heckling them or suggesting radical changes to the proposed plot. In the end, a consensus emerges between audience and the actors as to the play to be staged. But just as this is about to begin (Act 1 of the playlet coinciding with Act 1 of *On joue la comédie*), policemen swoop in yet again and, this time, arrest the actors. It is their subsequent fate and that of the policemen themselves that constitutes the rest of the published work, the playlet having been abandoned.

On joue la comédie displays a welcome formal consciousness that is absent from the predominant literary drama of francophone Africa. This is manifested in a variety of ways: in the way it constantly exhibits its fictionality, showing itself in the process of being made; in the way it destroys the 'realist illusion' by the continuous interruption of 'planted' actors (in the form of policemen and spectators); in its production techniques which require the action to be constantly commented on and announced in advance and the roles to be distributed on stage; in its manipulation of the face and the masque and so on.

To commentators like Tohonou Gbéasor and Denise de Saivre,[15] this consciousness betrays a strong Brechtian influence. While this is indeed quite possible (after all Zinsou took a postgraduate degree in modern European Drama in the University of Paris III, supervised by the noted drama critic Jean Schérer) there exists another source of inspiration, nearer home and freely admitted to by Zinsou himself. And that is the modern oral tradition of theatre known in Togo as the 'concert-party'.[16]

Of Nigerian and Ghanaian origin and arriving in Togo in the 1930s, the 'concert-party' in that country is an evening of musical and theatrical entertainment that sometimes lasts six hours. It divides into three parts: a warming-up session of music (mostly 'highlife'), song and dance, a prologue consisting of skits and story-telling whose beginning is signalled by the entry on stage of pierrot-like characters and finally an improvised play on social and moral issues. Performed in a mixture of languages (Ewe, Togo's lingua franca, French and pidgin-French) and tones (comic, satirical and burlesque) and interspersed with scenes of song and dance, the concert-party puts on stage stock characters: the 'houseboy', the 'charlatan', the 'prostitute' and so on. These are distinguishable by their conventional costumes, disguise, or make-up. Thus the 'prostitute' always wears bright, red lip-stick, sun glasses and an 'Afro' hair-style, while the 'houseboy' powders his face black with charcoal dust and carves out extra full lips from it with white chalk.[17]

The links between this popular oral tradition of theatre and *On joue* are many and I will deal with only the most salient. The first of these is the nature of their plots. The action in *On joue*, as the summary of it above shows, is, like that in a concert-party piece, totally improvised. With no written text and with only the broadest sketch of the storyline, the actors have to invent everything in the course of the actual performance: the dialogue, the plot, the acting. What one has in the end is not action that progresses logically in the tradition of the well-made play (which is precisely the complaint of one of the spectators within the play), but an open-ended structure *à la Waiting for Godot* to take a modern European example, where a series of vastly disconnected episodes – mostly to do with attempts to stage plays – revolve around a central character and his friends.

The danger of anarchy which haunts all such improvised theatre is reduced in the case of this play by the directing work of the Presenter, Xuma. Like his Togolese concert-party counterpart *le meneur de jeu*, (a kind of ringleader or producer), he controls both action and performers. He determines when a particular sequence has gone far enough and needs to progress. His various announcements ('now our play's going to start', p. 6; 'He's an actor', p. 11, referring to an old spectator; 'Don't be afraid of them, they aren't real policemen', p. 10, of the officers interrupting the play) are all meant to give some direction to the events, and help the spectator out of the confusion that might inevitably occur as a result of the constant shift from theatrical illusion to reality. Also the actors take their cue from him, breaking into song, mime or dance when he so directs. In addition to all this, he also distributes roles, as does the *meneur de jeu*. Thus after choosing the role of Chaka for himself at the end of the Prologue, he gives two fellow-actors the following instructions: 'You'll act N'koulou N'koulou ... And you'll disguise yourself as a woman to act Noliwé, Chaka's wife' (p. 19). The various roles distributed, he counsels his cast: 'Up to each one to play the part as he sees fit, as long as the outline is respected' (p. 20).

Another sense in which *On joue* derives much from the concert-party is in characterisation. In addition to the stereotypical nature of the characters (the warder, the policeman, the prisoner and so on) the play also has two of the common conventional types in concert-party dramas: the houseboy or 'master-boy' as he is called in that tradition and the old man. The former is represented by Xuma, the Presenter, who as Chaka in the playlet, *Chaka le messie* to be staged, has the distinctive costume of the 'master-boy': a pair of modern trousers over which is worn a torn pair of shorts, in this case a raffia mini-skirt. The latter is represented by the actor playing N'Koulou N'Koulou who wears the equally conventional white hair and beard. Female characters in the play, Noliwé and the female spectator who betrays Chaka (alias Xuma, the Presenter), are also played in concert-party tradition by men disguised as women.

The characters in *On joue* are also, like their counterparts in the popular tradition, all of modest origins. They are the antitheses of the exalted, princely figures of most ancient, oral tradition-based franco-phone plays. Expert at self-depreciation and conscious of only playing a part, they are more like clowns acting out circus numbers. And for this they rely not just on words, but significantly on mime, music and dance.

In keeping with their humble origins, their style of acting is consistently parodic. They ridicule just about everything; apartheid of course – the play's central concern – but also religion, themselves, foreign aid and, of particular interest to this article, a certain type of drama: the oral, histori-cal narrative-inspired heroic play with its debates, high seriousness and visionary heroes.

In the playlet, *Chaka le messie*, the solemnity, embodied in N'koulou N'koulou's tirades, is subverted by his comic appearance and tic, and by his envoy Chaka, who in his perpetual drunken state, reduces the entire production to comic proportions. Whenever N'koulou N'koulou attempts to be lyrical and highminded as befits a character in a Chaka play (p. 22), Chaka is ready in counterpoise with some unheroic response in colloquial language (p. 23).

A final feature of *On joue* derived from the concert-party play is the use of scenic space. The 'planted' actors technique used during the play (a device borrowed straight from the concert-party), the full use of various areas of the auditorium for the action, the singing and dancing in which the audience participate are all an attempt to establish a rapport between the latter and the actors on stage.

Zinsou's aesthetic of total participation of stage and audience in the construction of a play has ideological implications. Just as artistic creation should be the product of a collective endeavour and not the work of the Great Writer with the ready-made message, so social and political change (in the play, the fight against dictatorship) can only be brought about through an understanding of the issue by the wider public and its active involvement in the search for solutions. Both as an aesthetic and a politics, it is a radical departure from the more elitist post-colonial aesthetics and politics in Africa. It is in this sense and not in its content that *On joue la comédie* is, as the Presenter tells us, a truly 'revolutionary play' (p. 7).

The Problems of a Heritage

If modern French-language African drama has inherited themes, techniques and performance practices from the oral tradition both ancient and recent, it has also inherited some of the weaknesses of that tradition. One of these, critics point out,[18] is an elitist, epic view of history. Like his oral traditional predecessor and counterpart, the 'griot', the francophone dramatist does not only glamorise history, he reduces it almost exclusively to heroic deeds and wars. He sees it as the sole product of the actions of kings, queens or exceptional individuals to the total exclusion of the lives, actions and historical experiences of the common people.

In epic narratives as well as in many francophone plays, the people never figure as actors. The many exactions and depredations which they suffered at the hands of warring feudal chieftains were not considered subjects fit for epic song any more than their contemporary plight is considered fit for drama today. Now as in the past, they remain spectators who watch and submit passively, as the great decisions and actions affecting them are taken by a ruling class of exceptional individuals. Biodun Jeyifo sees this type of drama, which he describes as '"bourgeois" historical tragedy', and under which he specifically includes Soyinka's *Death and the King's Horseman* and, in footnote, Séydou Badian's *La mort de Chaka* as an instance of African drama in the service of an elite and not of the people:

> . . . the protagonist hero in these plays are scions of bourgeois individualism and solipsism: lone tragic heroes, proposed either as great historical personages or cultural heroes and avatars dominate the action; their connection to us is never dialectical; it is symbolic.[19]

While most francophone plays do indeed display an uncritical fascination with and an undemocratic view of the past, it should be said that not all of them indulge in such self-complacent narcissism. Plays like Dadié's *Béatrice du Congo* and *Iles de Tempête*, U'Tamsi's *Le Zulu*, Guy Menga's *La Marmite de Koka Mbala*, Zinsou's *On joue la comédie*, Oyono-Mbia's *Trois prétendants . . . un mari* and many more adopt a critical view towards the oral tradition either with regard to its history which is shown to have its fair share of villains, or its beliefs and practices, which are often portrayed as obscurantist.

Others still like U'Tamsi's *Le destin glorieux du Maréchal Nnikon Nniku*, Maxime Ndébeka's *Le Président*, *Equatorium*, Sony Labou Tansi's *La Parènthese de sang*, *Je soussigné cardiaque*, even turn their back on the predominant theme and angle of vision of the oral tradition altogether. They concentrate instead on what Soyinka calls 'the niggling, worrying, predictable present'[20] of sufferings and injustices.

But even if the weakness as mentioned above were true of *all* francophone drama, it would only be so in strictly *political* terms. A more relevant charge, artistic and not ideological, would be that with the exception of comedies, francophone plays are mostly undramatic. The construction of unified stories in which the interest of the spectator is aroused and tension is created and resolved through the development of a series of related situations, is not their 'forte'. Like the traditional performances from which they derive, they are more theatrical entertainments and spectacles than dramas.

An additional weakness of these plays, created by their excessive reliance on the oral tradition, is that of folklorism. While aspects of that tradition – music, song, dance, ritual ceremonies and so on – are, in the best plays, an integral part of the action, in others they remain artificial, a dispensable gesture to the demands of their foreign audience for the exotic.

These shortcomings notwithstanding, the oral tradition has enabled the francophone playwright to create a vital and original form of theatre.

NOTES

1. For earlier work on aspects of the relationship between the oral tradition (the ancient one, that is) and modern African drama in French see Mineke Schipper, *Théâtre et société en Afrique* (Abidjan-Dakar: Les Nouvelles Editions Africaines, 1984): 59–85 condensed in Mineke Schipper, 'Traditional Themes and Techniques in African Theatre and "Francophonie",' *Theatre Research International*, 9, 3 (1984): 215–32; F.X. Cuche, 'L'utilisation des techniques du théâtre traditionnel africain dans le théâtre négro-africain moderne', *Le théâtre négro-africain, Actes du Colloque d'Abidjan* (Paris: Présence Africaine, 1970): 137–42; Robert Cornevin, 'Théâtre et traditions africaines: Le mythe historique africain dans la tradition orale: son passage au théâtre, à la radio, à la télévision', *L'Afrique littéraire et artistique*, 54/55 (1979/80): 49–52; Ange-Séverin Malinda, 'Mythe et histoire dans le théâtre africain d'expression française', *Le Mois en Afrique*, 247–48 (1986): 116–26.
2. Hegel quoted by Ngũgĩ wa Thiong'o in *Homecoming* (London: Heinemann, 1972): 41.
3. On the historical consciousness of traditional African societies, see *inter alia* Boubou Hama and Joseph Ki-Zerbo, 'The Place of History in African Society', in *UNESCO General History of Africa 1*, ed. Joseph Ki-Zerbo (London: Heinemann, UNESCO, University of California Press, 1981): 43–52; Jan Vansina, 'Once Upon a Time: Oral Traditions as History in Africa', *Dedalus*, 100 (1971): 442–68; Jan Vansina, *Oral Tradition* (Harmondsworth: Penguin, 1965).
4. Ruth Finnegan, *Oral Literature in Africa* (London: OUP, 1970): 372.
5. Djibril Tamsir Niane, *Soundjata ou l'épopée mandingue* (Paris: Présence Africaine, 1960). Unless otherwise stated, all translations from the original French of texts in this article, critical as well as literary are by the present author.
6. On the historical theme in francophone drama, see Gary Warner, 'The Use of

Historical Sources in Francophone African Theatre', *Theatre Research International*, 9, 3 (1984): 180–94; Christophe Dailly 'L'Histoire', *Le Théâtre négro-Africain, Actes du Colloque d'Abidjan*: 87–93. For a helpful classification of francophone African plays according to themes see Harold Waters, *Black Theatre in French: A Guide* (Sherbrooke: Naaman, 1978), and his various updates in *World Literature Today*, 55, 3 (1981): 410–12; *World Literature Today*, 57, (1983): 43–8 and *Theatre Research International*, 9, 3 (1984): 195–215.

7. I am aware of the fact that 'legend' is a broad category and that as an oral narrative, it can be graded into 'historical', 'romantic' 'mythic' legend or epic, depending on its degree of historicity or fancy. For a subtle classification and characterisation of this oral art form, see Isidore Okpewho, *Myth in Africa* (London: CUP, 1983): 59–71. Isidore Okpewho, *The Epic in Africa* (New York: Columbia University Press, 1979); and Ruth Finnegan: 367–73.

8. Although Césaire is not African, his dramatic work *Une Saison au Congo* (Paris: Seuil, 1973) can be properly seen as belonging to the francophone African theatre, both in preoccupation and execution.

9. P.C. Oyie Ndzie, 'Le théâtre politique en Afrique noire et son expression dans la langue française', *Quel théâtre pour le développement en Afrique* (Dakar-Abidjan: NEA, 1985): 96.

10. On the griot in African theatre, see Lye Mu-daba Yoka, 'Le griot dans le théâtre africain', *Présence Francophone*, 13 (1976): 63–71.

11. For example, Michel Riffaterre, 'La syllepse intertextuelle', *Poétique*, 40 (1979): 496.

12. For a powerful statement of this position, see Kwasi Wiredu, *Philosophy and an African Culture* (London: CUP, 1980): 1–51.

13. Marie-José Hourantier, *Du rituel au théâtre-rituel* (Paris: Harmattan, 1984): 31.

14. Barthélémy Kotchy, 'New Trends in the Theatre of the Ivory Coast', *Theatre Research International*, 9, 3 (1984): 239.

15. See Tohonou Gbéasor, Preface to *On joue la comédie* (Haho/Haarlem, 1984): xvii and Denise de Saivre, 'Entretien avec Sénouvo Zinsou auteur togolais', *Recherche Pédagogie et Culture*, 57 (1982): 75.

16. Zinsou's acknowledgement of his debt to the 'concert-party' is contained in the interview to Denise de Saivre in Denise de Saivre: 75.

17. My account of the concert-party in Togo is based on personal experience of it 1984–88 and on the following studies: Alain Ricard, 'Réflexions sur le théâtre à Lomé, la dramaturgie du concert-party', *Recherche, Pédagogie, Culture*, 57 (1982): 63–70; Alain Ricard, 'Théâtre scolaire et théâtre populaire au Togo', *Revue d'Histoire Littéraire de France*, 1 (1975): 44–86; Alain Ricard, 'The Concert-party as a Genre: the Happy Stars of Lomé', *Research in African Literatures*, 2, 5 (1974): 165–179. On the concert-party in Nigeria and Ghana, see Joel Adedeji 'Le concert-party au Nigéria et les débuts d'Ogunde', and K.N. Bame 'Des origines et du développement du "concert-party" au Ghana' both articles in the *Revue d'Histoire Littéraire de France*, (1975) 21–25 and 10–20 respectively.

18. On the weaknesses of the oral tradition, see Lilyan Kesteloot's introduction to her edition of *Da Monzon de Segou: Epopée Bambara*, vol. 1 (Paris: Fernand Nathan, 1972); Biodun Jeyifo, 'Tragedy, History and Ideology' in Georg Gugelberger (ed.) *Marxism and African Literature* (London: James Currey, 1985).

19. Biodun Jeyifo, 'Tragedy, History and Ideology': 107.

20. Wole Soyinka, 'The Writer in a Modern African State' in Per Wastberg (ed.) *The Writer in Modern Africa* (Uppsala: The Scandinavian Institute of African Studies, 1968): 17.

Index